JE T'AIME... MAYBE?

JE T'AIME… MAYBE?

April Lily Heise

je t'aime me neither

JETAIMEMENEITHER.COM

JE T'AIME... MAYBE?

ISBN-13 : 978-0992005320
ISBN-10 : 0992005329

Cover Design by Aurélie Dhuit
www.aureliedhuit.com

Author photo by Rebecca Plotnick
www.rebeccaplotnick.com

Publisher:
TGRS Communications
21 Allen Avenue
Toronto, Ontario
Canada M4M 1T5

Email: jetaimemeneither@gmail.com
www.jetaimemeneither.com

This is a novelized memoir. All content is entirely based on reality, but is written in a storybook fashion because my life in Paris has slowly become an eccentric romance novel with its own set of princes and foes.

All names, and a handful of situations, have been altered in order to protect the reputations and identities of some of these rogue Romeos.

Bisous, Lily

CONTENTS

A SEDUCTIVE SPRINGTIME IN PARIS

ANTOINE [04/20/08 1:29 PM]
Bonjour! I will be in Montmartre all day!
It would be a pleasure to say hello in the
garden and to enjoy your sweet and
charming female presence.

"CLOSE YOUR EYES. Relax…" purred a smooth voice into my ear, its owner's lips gently grazing my cheek in the process. A fingertip delicately trailed down my left arm. Another hand airily traveled up my right, stopping for a moment to explore the delicate pocket of my elbow. Yet another breezed across my knee en route to my ankle while its twin gradually glided above it, then teasingly retreated once it had reached the boundary of my skirt.

"Take in the mutual pleasures of our radiant energies," he said in a hushed tone. My lips couldn't resist curling into a secret smile, however, my rational, panic-stricken mind could only keep asking: What the heck am I doing?! Or rather… What were they doing? I thought I'd agreed to a simple 'walk in the park'??

"That's right. We're here to serve your every desire," was his genie-like promise. A gentle gust of wind danced through the branches of the nearby trees, cuing a soft symphony of rustling leaves. This ethereal sonata only heightened the serene atmosphere.

I took a deep breath and slowly released my clenched eyelids. Their silky caresses continued over my face, arms and legs, some swooping daringly below my neck. One, two... now three pairs of sensual fingertips...

Oh la la! What had I gotten myself into this time?!

APRIL SHOWERS BRING...?

FROM: MARIO   Friday, April 4 2008 4:35 PM

Hi Lily,

Kinda strange receiving an email from me, right?
Things have changed on my end. I started working again
early February, in Nanterre, so not as interesting as
Nigeria, but I'm happy to be keeping busy.

I have also broken up with my girlfriend. It was not as
simple as that, but I am OK about it. I should be as it was
my decision.

I wanted to give you a call to discuss a few things with you,
is that okay? I thought I'd ask via email as that is less of a
shocker after so many months. Alternatively we can meet
for a coffee.

Mario

"DON'T WASTE a second on that deadbeat!" howled
Naughty, slamming down her glass on the table.

"A coffee? He owes you nothing less than dinner," scoffed
Pussycat, reaching for the bottle of champagne.

"In a Michelin-starred restaurant," added The Countess,
extending her empty glass towards Pussycat for a refill.

"Or if you *do* agree to see him, suggest rendezvousing near the Seine... so you can accidentally knock him into the river! That's the only place he belongs!" Naughty was getting really heated up. Hopefully some more bubbly would put out the flames sparked by mentioning Mario, the cause of the broken heart I'd been trying to mend over the last four months.

"Getting together... I mean, meeting up, might be therapeutic?" I timidly put forward.

"Or painfully reopen old wounds," warned Pussycat; Naughty and The Countess nodding silently in agreement. The girls were most certainly right and I should have guessed they wouldn't approve of me having anything at all to do with the sly Dutchman again.

I sighed and sought solace from effervescent Paris, a blurred twinkle shimmering on the other side of my glass, newly refilled with Domaine de Valentin champagne. Those lights dazzled with potential answers—or potential mischief—depending on your perspective. What was the opinion of the City of Love and Temptation on troublesome Mario?

Mario. He was the last in the disastrous series of bad boy stories that had put an end to my failed 'quest' to find a nice, light summer fling. A summer that turned into three years, much longer than even an Indian summer should last. From a guy whose girlfriend showed up on his doorstep with his baby to a lovesick military man who bombarded me with nonstop, passionate text messages and from an exciting encounter with a jet fighter pilot to trying to fight off a mistress-hunting married older man, these dozen or so romantic disasters eventually led me to Mario, a handsome Dutch-Canadian. I'd thought destiny had sent him as the fearless hero who would finally unlock the infernal chains constricting my heart. Sadly, he only starred as the antagonist in the grande finale of my cursed Greek-style romantic tragedy.

In all fairness, Mario wasn't the real problem. I was the only one to blame for attracting crazier upon crazier dating misadventures over time. I was letting myself aimlessly float along the River of Dead-End Relationships, taking little if no control over my makeshift raft. On many occasions, and with the wise advice of my best Parisian gal friends, I could have steered into safer waterways. Nevertheless, I rarely did. Sometimes we need to survive the storm or make our own way through the labyrinth in order to learn our lessons, just like those Greek heroes. At the end, as the chorus sung its resounding final notes, I'd come to the realization I would have to change my mindset and my behavior if I truly wanted to attract a serious relationship rather than the casual crap or absurdities I'd been luring in. Albeit occasionally very fun and/or funny, these stories were getting me nowhere on the love front. I might have been ready to alter my line of thinking; all the same, I still had to contend with the fervent amorous energy of Paris, which was often a powerful force to be reckoned with.

Indeed, much more had happened in these last few months. This spring marked my seven-year anniversary of living in Paris. How young and innocent I'd been back then, fresh out of university from small-town Canada, embarking for Paris—the city of my dreams. The French capital had completely won my heart during my semester abroad here the previous year and I couldn't help going in pursuit of this new love immediately after graduating. Once arrived, I quickly succeeded in getting a job teaching business English, for a school I later found out was run by Scientologists! I'd only intended to teach for a year, maximum eighteen months. It was supposed to be my gateway to residing here; after a teaching stint to get myself on my feet, I'd surely find the perfect cool job to apply my art degree to. Yet, upon discovering the news about the horrible cult my bosses belonged to, and that my work permit might be transferable to another company, I instantly started my job search. This professional quest took up virtually all my free time. That is, when I wasn't hanging out with my fabulous gang of girlfriends.

Despite the countless applications I sent in reply to interesting job ads, these never managed to get past the close-minded barricade most French employers had erected on the job front. Everyone in the French work world seemed to be thrown into a specific professional box according to one's degree (or one's first job), and as a result, you were condemned to rot in that particular career hell. Forever. I even tried to get in at a few of the companies I taught at; surely these students recognized my capabilities, having gotten to know me during our lessons. Nevertheless, for them, I was just 'an English teacher' with an art degree from a distant university with an unpronounceable name they'd never heard of. I should have just given up and put that on a business card.

After a year and a half I managed to escape the clutches of the Scientologists (much to their dismay) and, by jumping through various Work Visa hoops, and compiling a forest-worth of paperwork for the préfecture, I was able to stay on in France. Over the years I did find some alternative work, but my main *baguette et beurre* was still teaching. I was getting older and with the passing years came a sentiment that sacrificing my career for the sake of merely being in my dream city was no longer enough. I eventually gave up on finding a traditional French job and, since the beginning of the year, I'd taken matters into my own hands. *Au revoir* to the present perfect, confusing prepositions and complicated idiomatic expressions: I was returning to tourism.

I'd worked in some art galleries and had been a museum guide as a student back in Canada, plus my first job in France was as a guide at an important Canadian WWI memorial. Then, while I was awaiting my Visa to work for the Scientologists, I donned the hat of tour director for traveling groups of high school students. At least tourism was a decent conduit for my passion for France, its history and culture and, in its own way, to art in general. Paris was a living museum after all.

Knowing of my desire to switch careers, Mademoiselle Sécret, a travel writer and tour guide friend of mine, started referring me to various guiding opportunities. As these were quickly picking up, I was able to gradually ease out of teaching, to the point where I only kept a few well-paid or interesting classes. The tours, in addition to the occasional translation project, could comfortably sustain me.

Now here we were in spring, the season that's meant for growth and bringing forth new things. The professional seeds I'd been planting were starting to blossom—so, could other areas of my life also begin to flourish? Romance was definitely blooming, but in someone else's garden. Our dear friend Special Kay, the pretty, enthusiastic Californian who'd been the fourth musketeer in our little Parisian expat quartet, was in love. She'd met her *homme parfait*, the best friend of the boyfriend of Cindy, another good friend of ours. After pining after her boss' evil son for many years, she was ready to move on to real love. It seemed like she'd found it and she was completely head over heels for her Frenchie. This was proof that meeting *Monsieur Parfait* in Paris was actually possible.

However, this also meant, at least for the time being, that we'd 'lost' her to the land of *amour*. Usually, when expats living abroad 'lose' their friends it's because they've moved back home. We hoped Kay would make her way out of her romantic vortex and still hang out with us from time to time—which she gradually did—though rarely without her beau. Therefore, we needed a new *fille* to join our little crew which included two other fellow Canadians: Naughty, a lively dance student from Toronto who was finishing up her

Master's at the *Conservatoire de Paris* and Pussycat, a spunky photographer from Montréal trying to break into the Parisian fashion scene.

In a way, it was fortuitous timing that I'd just met a big group of fun foreigners, thanks to volunteering for a local film festival—yet another of my job search ploys. The festival mightn't have lead to a job, but it did inadvertently lead to meeting The Countess. Well, she wasn't a real 'countess'; she was Irish and thus naturally anti-aristocracy, due to her country being dominated by authoritative British lords for centuries. She'd received her nickname because she simply radiated refinement and class, but had a heart of pure fun. She'd recently moved to Paris after living in Madrid for a number of years where she'd taught English and had been engaged to an important Spanish doctor. When the engagement fell through, she exchanged bourgeois parties in the Iberian capital for hobnobbing with top executives in Paris at her new killer job working for a large international banking group. Her long hours came with the reward of a private chauffeur service, business trips to exotic lands, and a salary to afford the best champagnes. As such, The Countess' apartment in the trendy Marais district with a view overlooking l'Hotel de Ville, the Paris City Hall, and the towers of Notre Dame Cathedral, replaced my smaller abode, in less central Montmartre, as our new hangout. However, as cool as her place was, perhaps I should have been concerned by spending too much time on her street: rue des Mauvais Garçons (Bad Boys Street).

That particular night we were celebrating her recent promotion. This had come with a substantial raise and two bottles of bubbly—le Domaine de Valentin, which was slowly ousting our go-to red wine, le Saint Amour, as our new favorite beverage of choice. I'd just popped the second of the two hoping this would distract the girls from the uncomfortable conversation about Mario that we were still in the thick of.

"Why is he writing to you now? He must want something besides just a 'coffee,' don't you think?" analyzed Naughty.

"He's probably afraid of running into us at the pub or other expat events," deducted Pussycat.

"He'd get a royal lynching, that's for sure!" declared The Countess.

I tended to agree with them. He obviously had some ulterior motive other than forgiveness. That is, unless he'd joined a church (Scientology?) and was compelled to redeem his sins.

"Well, only one way to find out... *right?*" I mused timidly, looking around the room for some support, only to find three sets of rolling eyes and shaking heads. There was no point in me trying to convince them. Since it didn't seem like they were going to budge, I certainly wasn't going to tell them the *whole* truth. I'd actually already replied to Mario... but they need not fear: he wasn't the only *garçon* I'd been receiving messages from...

Since spring had recently sprung, it was the perfect time to turn over a new leaf, what I truly hoped seeing Mario would thereafter allow me to do. Over these last few months, I'd managed to wean myself off thinking about him; now he only entered my thoughts once or twice a week. I'd already understood that nothing was meant to happen with him, but my heartbeat still quickened as I clicked into his email suggesting to speak by phone or meet up for a coffee.

The day after receiving his unexpected message, I sent him a short reply agreeing to a drink—coffee wasn't going to cut it! I'd need a glass of wine to calm my nerves if I was going to see him in person. Later that day, as I was getting out of the *métro*, my phone buzzed with a missed call from him. *Yikes!* I'd only just accepted to see him, but I wasn't prepared to actually 'speak' to him yet. I needed to ease into the idea, and digital communication seemed the best avenue, plus I had to try to maintain the upper hand and keep a cool tone, something I was normally incapable of doing with my chipper voice and upbeat attitude. My optimism and kindness were the source of much of the trouble I found myself in. So I replied by text message, offering up a day for us to meet.

MARIO [04/08/08 3:16 PM]
OK see you tomorrow
outside the metro at 6:00 pm.

In our text message exchange, we settled on rendezvousing outside *métro* Blanche, a few blocks from my place. It was his idea to meet, therefore he should be the one making more of an effort by coming to my neck of the woods. Still, I didn't want to be too close to home, in case he actually did have other... intentions.

Spring is usually a glorious time in Paris with balmy sunny days brightening up spirits after a long, grey and rainy winter. This spring was no exception and I could already sense the improved attitude of the Parisians. I normally would have been equally thrilled by the wonderful weather, however, on that particular day I feared it would be counterproductive to my intention of coming across as chilly and reserved towards Mario.

I purposely went down to meet him a few minutes late. He deserved to wait, even for just a short time. There he was, as cute as ever. I reminded myself of my pledge to let neither his good looks nor his Dutch accent have any effect on me. After a quick *bise* cheek-kiss greeting, we went in search of the nearest sun-soaked terrace, as it was simply too nice to sit inside. This happened to be one of our old haunts: O'Hooligans. It was probably the first time I'd been to this Irish pub-dance club before midnight, where the girls and I had spent many an evening dancing until dawn while fending off (or inviting in) flirtatious boys.

After a few sips from our glasses of wine, he cut straight to the chase of why he wanted to see me. Pussycat had guessed it right.

As he was starting to get back on the dating scene, he pretty much wanted to make sure I wouldn't cause him any trouble. I wish he hadn't brought it up so early in our conversation; he'd caught me completely off guard and I couldn't do much besides stammer a few vague promises I wouldn't do anything embarrassing if I ran into him and a would-be conquest. Any proper chastising would have to wait until later.

We moved on to other topics and the thick tension from when we first met up began to dissipate with our friendlier chatter. The emptying of wine glasses gave way to an awkward 'What are we going to do now?' moment. He suggested dinner, and I agreed. While it wouldn't be the Michelin-starred meal The Countess affirmed I merited from him, it seemed too depressing to just go home, plus I hadn't gotten everything off my chest. We went up to nearby rue des Abbesses, lined with lively cafés, and found another table *en terrasse*. Here, tensions eased even more (I was miserable at playing tough!) and the fluidity of our conversation became as smooth as the Burgundy in our glasses.

"So, coming back to Paris after the Christmas holidays I was on the same flight as your friend, the one with short dark hair…" Mario started rather cheerfully, digging into his steak-frites.

"Naughty."

"Yep, that's the one. I wasn't sure if I should say Hi."

"It's a good thing you didn't because she probably would have punched you."

A verbal blow, though much lighter than the physical one Naughty probably would have administered.

"I guess I would have deserved it," he resigned.

That was just the invitation I needed to bring up the matter of his poor behavior—the few glasses of wine I'd already consumed had strengthened my courage. Calm but critical, I tore him apart for having repeatedly cheated on his girlfriend (with me and possibly others), leaving out the personal damage done to me by leading me on and stamping on my heart. Once my onslaught was over, he shamefully acknowledged his wrongdoing and claimed that when he found his real soul mate, he'd give her his 200% and more *blah, blah, blah.*

Even if his declarations proved mere empty promises, it felt good to confront him and not let him off scot-free. I didn't get complete justice (he didn't end up at the bottom of the Seine like the sentence Naughty had judged appropriate for his love crimes). Actually, the most useful part of seeing him was my coming to the realization that we had quite different values, underscoring the fact we were just not a good match.

Perhaps it really wasn't fate that had propelled us together, but the passions of Paris. The romantic power of the City of *Amour*—teasing and tantalizing, seductive and sultry—often won over reason. It wasn't just its picture-perfect cityscape; there truly was a vivacious amorous ardor underlying so much of what happened here. However, on this very night, it would not dominate. I could now shed myself of the alluring Dutchman and move on.

Move on... *to whom?*

Mario deftly steered the subject away from his misdemeanors by asking me if I was seeing anyone. I highly doubted he had any other hidden motives behind his question and I especially didn't want to look like the pathetic loser in all of this either, so told him there were a few prospects on my horizon. This wasn't a fib either: the romantic wheels of Paris where turning in other directions that week as well...

> JACQUES [04/09/08 5:42 PM]
> Hello Boss! I'm coming to town
> next week, how about dinner?

Sigh! The very next day after Mario had sent me his first email, I received an SMS from the other problematic love interest from the end of last year: Jacques, an international man of mystery, or rather *husband* of mystery! He had a very intriguing profile, though I wondered where his collection of wives was currently hiding. Had they gone into hibernation for the winter?

Another blast from the past. What about that *new* leaf? How could I move on when these old autumn leaves kept blowing onto my path, obscuring my vision and casting a shadow on my new prospects?

No big surprise from Jacques. He was doing his usual breeze into and, almost as soon, out of town magic act. I wasn't really sure I wanted to see him. Winter hadn't been completely icy cold. I'd actually been tempted by Jacques' dinner invitations a couple of times; however, the last time I'd accepted, over our meal he started on with these world domination conspiracy theories… not at all appetizing conversation nor romantic prospects. Besides that, he still wasn't very clear about his mysterious ex-or-not wife/wives. This shadiness made me trust him—and want to date him seriously—even less.

Maybe I could just pretend I hadn't received his text message? My finger hovered above the delete button, instead it clicked into my phone preferences where I changed my screensaver to a photo of a bright, spring garden full of vibrant flowers. I then turned my focus towards attracting the right person into my life. Some positive visualization could help draw some new amorous energy in my direction. At the very least, it couldn't hurt, right?

ANTOINE [04/20/08 1:29 PM]
Bonjour! I will be in Montmartre all day!
It would be a pleasure to say hello in the
garden and to enjoy your sweet and
charming female presence.

Uh-oh! I'd forgotten about the danger of putting out too many love vibes… it can really work!

Antoine was a Frenchman based in Madrid, when he wasn't galavanting around the world from Kiev to Caracas. We'd met a few years back at an international social mixer, and he would drop me the occasional text message when he was back in Paris. One would be hard up to find someone more charismatic, adventurous or with such a *puuurrrrfectly* seductive voice. So why hadn't I been dating him instead of all of these problematic suitors over the years? Unfortunately, his sex appeal stopped at the amazingly titillating words he uttered. It wasn't that the mid-to-late thirty-something blond was unattractive. I just felt no romantic chemistry between us.

The last time he'd been in Paris, we grabbed a drink in my neighborhood and took what should have been a terribly romantic stroll through the dimly lit, narrow cobblestone streets of Montmartre. It was like the spirits of centuries of departed lovers floated through the area, compelling people to kiss. At one moment, I even thought he was going to try just that—but possibly sensing my unreceptiveness—he backed off.

At the time, my mind was likely all muddled up with one of the useless guys taking his turn at clouding my better romantic judgment. Sometimes our perspectives can change when our mindset does. Was the timing right now? Perhaps if we could spend a little more time to get to know each other, flames could spark? Sure, I'd hoped to turn over a 'new leaf,' that didn't necessarily mean it had to be with a new person as long as we hadn't already dated, did it?

Of romantic interest or not, I thoroughly enjoyed Antoine's delightful company. The sun was shining, and he'd proposed meeting right around the corner from my place. How could I say *non*? I wasn't expecting anything besides spending the afternoon in a lovely setting with interesting people.

Rounding the corner towards Sacré Coeur, the elaborate, white basilica crowning Montmartre, the 'Mountain of the Martyrs,' it was easy to spot Antoine lounging on the steps underneath the lacy church, avidly chatting with two unknown boys. Getting a little closer, I almost stopped dead in my tracks.

Oh la la! Who was he with? The first one looked like an average French guy, but the second... was the spitting image of Adrien Brody! I adored this offbeat actor; while I knew it was highly doubtful that it was actually him in the flesh and blood, I'd take this younger look-alike!

On weak knees, I wavered the remaining ten steps to reach them. In my stupor, I vaguely foresaw that the afternoon would be anything but an average sunny afternoon with friends... it might even involve more than one *sacred heart.*

"*Voilà! La charmante demoiselle* has arrived," welcomed Antoine, spryly springing to his feet and bestowing me with a knightly bow.

After *bonjours* and *bises* were exchanged all around, the men filled me in on their afternoon mission. They were playing 'tourist for a day in Paris' by filming silly video sketches about getting to know the city—exactly the sort of quirky idea Antoine would come up with. Since they were all French, I gathered they were hoping I'd play the part of the unwitting foreign tourist. I'd happily accept the role as long as I would be starring alongside Adrien Brody!

Action!

"Isn't Paris *magnifique*..." declared Adrien looking out at the impressive view of the city beheld from Sacré Coeur's perch.

"Yes, it's soooo... romantic!" I murmured, staring deep into Adrien's beautiful brown eyes. Forget those grey rooftops! The romance could be right here!

Pretty soon the real tourists—snapping photos of that idyllic view or selfies with the mammoth white church—were getting distracted by our goofy antics and giving us funny looks. This just sent us into bigger fits of laughter, which caused an ever bigger disturbance. I took out an invisible film clapper and shouted 'cut,' suggesting we take a little break from our film-capades in the little park behind Sacré Coeur— we'd certainly make less of a 'scene' there. However, the change of setting didn't put an end to our video: this shifted to fake interviews with 'Mr. Brody' (I obviously wasn't the only one who'd noticed his resemblance to the famous actor). Soon enough our giggles forced us to call a wrap to all filming. We collapsed under the vine-laden arcade, which bordered one edge of the park, an even more romantic setting than in front of the basilica...

"Close your eyes. Relax..." Antoine purred into my ear once seated under the shady pergolas.

I innocently obeyed, not having the slightest idea what he might be up to. He possibly didn't either, but he was quick on his feet... or in this case... his hands.

Before I could even fathom what was happening, delicate fingertips were softly tracing paths up and down any visible patches of my skin, being clad in my usual skirt and top attire and with the weather being so nice, there was plenty of open terrain for them to travel on! There were definitely more fingertips than could all belong to Antoine—unless he'd magically turned into a many-handed Hindu god! One, two, three sets of seductive hands... and one pair certainly belonged to Adrien Brody!

Oh la la! What had I gotten myself into this time?!

The fairy-like fingertips continued their delicate and somewhat daring waltz until it was finally broken by a question:

"Mommy, what are they doing to her?" The voice could only be that of a young girl. My eyes sprung open and the spell was broken. Even though I couldn't see what they had been doing, I could easily envision how this could have looked to passers-by. The French did not shy away from public displays of affection; however, this was in an entirely different category, one which certainly must have had the saints and the sacred heart linked to the church, frowning down from heaven.

We all needed to cool down (in more ways than one), so we made our way to a neighborhood convenience store for ice creams, which I suggested we could eat back at my place. I made some ice tea to go with our *glaces*, hoping this would assist in the chilling process, but I shouldn't have been all that surprised when the caressing treatment began again.

Did these guys have something *more* in mind? I couldn't help thinking back to when I was a naïve twenty-two-year-old backpacking around Spain (just before starting to my contract with the Scientologists) and these three Argentinians I'd met in Madrid tried to get me to have a foursome with them. Although they were unsuccessful, I'd only narrowly escaped that one. Ever since, I'd tried to be extra cautious about these sorts of 'group' situations, yet today I'd walked straight into it!

I only wanted to meet ONE decent guy... Not THREE!

Had this all been my fault for having sent out those love vibes last week? Was I putting too much out into the universe? Ask for love in Paris and thou shalt receive, though why can't it just be in the form thou hath had in mind?

In all truth I wasn't terribly fond of the third guy; he was the one getting a little too cheeky with the caresses and exuded a certain degree of sliminess. Just as I was thinking I would have to put a stop to their less-than-tame and now less-than-public displays of affection and what could evolve into them trying to film a B-grade erotic movie (was that what they'd really had in mind with their shooting in Montmartre? 'Red Light Lily'?), Antoine's cell chimed. Saved by the bell.

"*Ah, c'est vrai.* We have an appointment with Pierre at Place des Abbesses, and we're late," he reminded the third guy. The 'we' appeared to be just Antoine and Mr. Cheeky.

"I'll come back to pick up Adrien a little later," he promised and off the two of them fled, with Mr. Cheeky trying to find an excuse to get my number. *Non, ce n'est pas possible.* I was sure that he wasn't the answer to my dating prayers... however, it had seemed that a God up in the sky *had* been listening! I was now alone with Adrien Brody! *Oh mon Dieu! Had my Messiah arrived?*

We were trying to be serious after Antoine and Mr. Cheeky left. He pulled out his phone and showed me the klezmer instrument he played (ah ha! He was indeed Jewish like the real Adrien... and cute *and* talented!). Then he showed me his photo on the European Jewish Student Association website, of which he was the Vice President (add smart and ambitious to the list!). Holy Moses!

Possibly distracted by his greatness, I didn't notice right away that he returned to caressing my arm, which turned into my thigh and my side... All this sensuality had gotten him a bit too excited. I wasn't going to find out if he was circumcised, at least not that exact day. I might never get the chance to kiss Adrien Brody again, but that's where I put on the brakes. After a while he had to run off to meet his brother, but he asked for my number. I was truly hoping he'd give me a call... well, when he got back from the American Jewish Congress he was attending the following week.

The next week came and went then another and another. Sadly, it seemed my true Messiah hadn't actually come. I'd have to keep on wandering, but the revitalizing and *new* romantic energy of spring had given me hope and helped turn over that new leaf after all.

Lily la Tigresse appeared to be back in business, and she was on the hunt for her true soul mate!

PICNICS, POSTCARDS
AND MONSIEUR PARFAIT

LIONEL [06/12/08 9:29 PM]
Thanks for another lovely evening. Good
luck tomorrow and I hope to see you very
soon... I hope this week-end. Good night
charming mademoiselle.

THIS YEAR'S SPRING in Paris was turning out to be a beautiful one, and this particular Sunday was exceptionally warm and sunny. It was perfect weather for picnicking and it just so happened that I was going to be spending the afternoon doing just that, the first of what I'd hope to be many throughout the season. It was being held to celebrate the birthday of Charles, the French husband of our friend Céline, who was also from Québec like Pussycat. The one tiny downside was that the park we'd be camping out at was in the suburbs where they lived. The suburbs. *Uggh.* It was a destination us all-too-*Parisienne*-Canadian gals generally avoided like the plague.

NAUGHTY [05/05/08 11:30 AM]
Meet you on the RER platform at 12:30 pm?

PUSSYCAT [05/05/08 12:05 PM]
Merde, which train line is it on??

NAUGHTY [05/05/08 12:40 PM]
Coming!!!!

Pussycat was firmly anti-suburbs, while Naughty was firmly perpetually late… the two challenges combined made us arrive at the very, very fashionably late time of 1:30 pm instead of scheduled invite time of 12:30 pm. Oh well, better late than never!

The three of us eventually arrived at the Rueil-Malmaison suburban train station and attempted to find our way to the town's main attraction: Le Chateau de Malmaison. The 18th-Century castle and estate once belonged to Napoléon and Joséphine Bonaparte and was one of their favorite residences. When Napoléon was off trying to conquer all of Europe, he wrote frequent, fervently passionate letters to Joséphine, which she'd surely read in her prized garden located behind the *château*, at the time considered one of the most beautiful on the continent. Wasn't it the perfect setting for a Napoléon-sized romance?

Finally arriving at the park, we entered through its grand gates and went in search of our picnickers, whom we found spread out under a large, shady tree. In doing the obligatory round of arrival *bises* kisses to absolutely everyone, I noticed that there were many people we didn't know, certainly friends of Charles who'd come out for his birthday. We eked out a section of blanket for ourselves next to Céline, added our lunch contributions to the communal cornucopia and helped ourselves to some rosé, well-deserved after our epic commute.

We mostly remained in our girl clique, catching up on everyone's respective news and nibbling on pieces of cheese and quiche, so I'd hardly noticed the potentially dateable boys whose cheeks we must have previously kissed until we were cutting into the birthday cake.

"Some champagne to go with your cake?" offered a friendly voice. I looked up from my chatting with the girls to find the smile of one of Charles' friends, Lionel, bottle of bubbly in hand.

"*Merci!*" I cheerfully accepted, holding out my glass.

Lionel took this opportunity to have a seat next to me. This was actually the first time Céline had mixed her friends with her husband-to-be's group. Had Charles been hiding a potential catch?

Sweet and enthusiastic, Lionel struck up a pleasant conversation with me which went beyond the trite 'What are you doing in France?' spiel we were used to. Pretty soon he knew all about the small town I'd grown up in and I got to hear about his exciting upcoming travels for work.

"Thailand! Wow! I've always wanted to go!" I marveled.

"I could send you a postcard, if you like?" He kindly volunteered.

"Sure, that'd be great, that's probably as close as I'll get to going myself."

As the sun crept lower in the sky and the cool spring evening air set in, we began to wrap up our splendid *pique-nique*. On our way out of the park's gilded gates, Lionel stopped me:

"Why don't you text me your address for that postcard?" he suggested, slyly obtaining my number as well as my address.

Apparently romance really did still emanate from the Imperial Gardens...

The month of May can be a fickle one in Paris. The spectacular sunny skies we'd had up to the day of the picnic were about to be covered in a brooding grey cast that refused to budge for the rest of the month. Although the Gods were depriving us of the sunshine, a special dose was delivered to me personally by the mailman—in the form of a postcard. I turned it over to find the sunny port of... *Marseille?* Who'd gone to Marseille?

> Salut Lily,
> If you've never been to Marseille, you have to add it to your travel list.
> For the city, the Calanques and for the wonderful views of the bay.
> This is my "test card" to gage the speed of the Thai, Malaysian and French postal services!
> Lionel

Wow! Lionel! He hadn't forgotten his promise! What's this about the Thai AND Malaysian postal services? More cards were certainly on their way. I was glowing and completely charmed. What a sweetheart, I thought.

My Thai postcard arrived a few days later, but before any others appeared, I received news from Lionel via a faster means of communication.

LIONEL [06/02/08 7:35 PM]
Anything interesting in your mailbox? ;-)

That little cutie. He couldn't wait any longer!

LIONEL [06/02/08 9:12 PM]
Postcards... 2 out of 3! It would be nice to
meet up for a drink. It's already a bit late
tonight... can I call you during the week?

Phone call made. Date set. Things were on the right track! For the first time in months my heart was starting to thaw. Lionel seemed both nice and attentive: could he have real potential?

LIONEL [06/08/08 10:53 PM]
Merci, I had a marvelous evening.
I'll give you a call to see if we can
do something Thursday. Sweet dreams.

Lionel had brought back the sun along with his last postcard. The cobblestones were shimmering in the late afternoon sun as I made my way to our rendezvous point near the lively rue Montorgueil market street, packed with café terraces, *boulangeries* wafting the aromas of fresh baguettes and fishmongers loudly hawking the last of the catch of the day. It was one of my favorite areas of Paris, this would surely be a good omen for our date, *n'est pas?*

I caught sight of Lionel as I was approaching. What did he have in his hands? Were those... *flowers?!*

"And that's not all!" He exclaimed with a playful grin, producing first one then a second package from behind his back. Gleeful surprise must have been written all over my face. I carefully unwrapped his packages to reveal two beautiful raw silk scarves.

"I couldn't decide which one best matched your pretty green eyes... so I got you both!" he really had been thinking of me while he was away in Thailand. I was utterly shocked, and seriously impressed.

We found a sunny terrace for *apéro* and started catching up. Over our *kirs* of white Burgundy Aligoté wine and *crème de cassis*, I got to hear about his latest work adventures around the globe. There were more to come, he informed me, as in the next few weeks he'd be traveling much closer to home, to various places around France. He told me a bit more about his job and, from what I understood, he worked as a consultant for an engineering company. Even though his work didn't sound terribly exciting, it certainly took him to some fascinating places.

Glasses now empty, he suggested moving on to an Italian restaurant he knew, located on a nearby side street. The restaurant was even tinier than the street it was on, containing perhaps a dozen or so tables for two, its walls covered in tasteful Italian vintage posters and photographs. It was the perfect place for a first date, but would there be a second?

LIONEL [06/12/08 9:29 PM]
Thanks for another lovely evening. Good luck tomorrow and I hope to see you very soon... I hope this week-end. Good night charming mademoiselle.

"It sounds like he really likes you!" squealed Naughty.

"First three postcards," started Pussycat. "Then two gifts AND flowers?"

"Were the scarves *real* silk?" asked The Countess, keeping up her usual high standards. We were all over at The Countess' apartment, seated in a line so we could all enjoy her spectacular view. Hotel de Ville was showing off in the sun and the bells of Notre Dame were tolling to announce evening mass. We were communing with our rosé wine and confessing our latest gossip.

"Well, I was definitely caught off guard!" I replied.

"Just caught off guard?" questioned Naughty with a raised eyebrow. "You weren't entirely swept off your feet?"

"Ummm... maybe swept off... one foot?" It was apparent from the stern look mirrored in all of the girls' eyes that they did not approve of my answer.

There was no question, Lionel had thoroughly wowed me with his thoughtfulness. His charm and enthusiasm were contagious. However, there was something holding me back.

Was it the wariness I'd acquired from three years of romantic disappointments, or something else?

Lionel was absolutely adorable, but in that kind of little brother of your best friend way. I couldn't have come across a sweeter, kinder person. However, I also had this nagging feeling that he was just a tad too… normal.

An engineer, a graduate of a French *'grande école'* ivy-league university, he went to see his family back in Brittany whenever he could and was probably saving up for a nice house in a Parisian suburb, run impeccably by a future model wife who was raising his 2.01 children (the average in France). There is positively nothing wrong with this. On the contrary, this was all great. It just wasn't me.

At all.

'Normal' would be the last adjective to describe my childhood.

"I wasn't a hippie," my mom used to say. "People think hippies are dirty."

Okay, fine, my mother was a clean young woman wearing bellbottoms and had flowers braided into her hair. It's true, she wasn't a full-fledged hippie, but she'd embraced a back-to-the-land approach, which had drawn her to the countryside, hours away from any city, where many other 1970s free-spirits had settled. It was here where I was born, in a house, in the middle of the fields and forests. Lily of the Valley.

It didn't take me all that long to realize we were a little different from the 'others' in our town and for a long time growing up I tried to be anything but that. I was a well-behaved, model straight-A student, I volunteered for associations and was on student council. However, in high school I started to diverge off the straight and narrow; I got involved in theater, began pursuing art more seriously and became a vegetarian; activities and actions which were more connected to my offbeat upbringing. Traveling to Italy on exchange when I was seventeen and seeing the phenomenal works of Michelangelo, Raffaello and da Vinci in person, helped swing the balance in art's favor.

In the end, I did go to art school instead of law school, which had been my dream back in my 'serious' days. My rebellious spirit persisted, but now with a sophisticated European edge, one that was further accentuated by spending three months here in university. Paris seemed to be the best place for me. It was where my two personalities could co-exist, and in fact, they were almost the 'norm' in this eccentric yet elegant city.

Considering the above, I was more attracted to men who had a little *je ne sais quoi*. I didn't think I could properly relate to someone who wasn't at least a little out-of-the-ordinary or quirky in some way or another. They may have also had an unusual upbringing, they may have spent a year backpacking around the world, or perhaps they'd had an intriguing life in some other way; they just had to have some edge. That said, too atypical was often disastrous. Therefore, I was hoping to find someone who was a little 'outside the box,' though not completely from another planet.

This is why I had an inkling that Lionel might be too square. He did travel a lot, but this was for work, not out of choice. Geez, perhaps I was being too quick to judge? Just because he was an engineer, didn't mean he didn't have some originality.

> LIONEL [06/15/08 8:29 PM]
> Salut Lily. Do you want to do something
> tomorrow? Maybe we could go to the
> movies? Just let me know. Ciao

A few days after our first date, we did go out again, this time for dinner and a movie. He was so nice and vivacious; it was impossible to not have an enjoyable evening with him, although I was beginning to wonder if I could have stronger feelings for him other than friendship. I was mulling this over the next day when I saw my Facebook inbox flashing with a new message.

From: Viktor   Monday, June 16 2008 6:42 PM

Hey Lily,
From Peterborough? I wonder what you are up to these days? I am working out of Vancouver, but spending time in Germany, Russia and Marseille, France for work.

Don't ask me how I found you, but have some great memories at Guelph with you.

Viktor

My jaw dropped. Viktor. The one who'd gotten away…

I can't remember exactly how and when Viktor and I had met, but it was likely at an exhibit opening party at the gallery located in my Art School building. These very sociable wine-filled evenings tended to draw in students from other departments. Born and raised in South-West Africa, current day Namibia, Viktor came from a line of colonial farmers who'd stayed on in the country after its independence in 1990. Sandy blond hair and sparkling blue eyes, English was his mother tongue, but he sported the sexiest accent. He'd come to Canada for his studies and had somehow ended up at our certainly little-known-abroad, mid-sized university.

In my last year, I seemed to run into Viktor much more frequently. Was he going out of his way to see me? While it mightn't have been a lightning bolt love at first sight, I was highly fond of him. It seemed like the feelings were mutual, as gradually over the course of that last semester Viktor started dropping the slyest comments whenever we were alone. The flirt-o-meter rose and rose. He was even due to stop by the dingy student apartment I shared with my friend Wilhelmina one evening and said he hope I'd answer the door in some sexy lingerie. I didn't go that far, but I did have a cute, lacy red top on. Did he try anything? Nope. He went back into his shell, like all the times I countered his flirtations with a saucy reply, which drove me totally crazy. This carried on for the remaining few months of our studies, and then he was gone. The last I knew, he'd gone off to Thailand to teach diving or something exotic like that. As such, I had always remembered him as one of the few boys in my life's trajectory that had missed love's destined mark...

I hadn't heard from him since we'd left university. Was he now coming back into my life, albeit virtually to start? Regardless of what might or mightn't happen, it would be nice to see what he was up to. With curiosity, I sent a detailed reply with a summary of what was going on in my life.

From: Viktor   Monday, June 16 2008 8:08 PM

Hey Lily,

I still remember that one art project where you had to trace your outline. Are you still in the art scene?

I am actually in Marseille at the moment until the end of the week. I will likely be back every few months - perhaps August or September this year. Paris sounds like fun - although I am sure that your French is better than mine.

Great hearing from you.

Viktor

He was in... MARSEILLE? What odd timing for him to be inspired to write me, when he was a mere three-hour train ride away. This had to be destiny's wheels turning!

From: Viktor   Monday, June 16 2008 8:49 PM

Hey,
The weather down here has been pretty crappy too. My plan to visit a nude beach has been foiled, although I am not sure that I could "relax" enough to really enjoy it. I am a big fan of skinny dipping out West, but it is usually in great seclusion, and have never done it around other people, so don't have to worry about what kind of wood I sport.

You definitely have a very busy life it seems. I will have to work in Paris the next time. Give me a ring when you are in Vancouver. Would be great to see you again.

Xoxo Viktor

He was so close, I was seriously toying with the idea of jumping on the next high speed train south. Okay, not to go to the nudist beach, but I'd be fine with some private… nudism.

From: Viktor   Monday, June 16 2008 9:24 PM

How ironic. Was just looking through your South Africa pics - beautiful. I was there three times last year, most likely in Cape Town, Langebaan and the Wine Country almost exactly the same time as you!

The messages just kept coming and with more coincidences! This was killing me! Why hadn't he contacted me last year? We could have been catching up over some delicious South African wine in Cape Town… or why not, skinny dipping in the gorgeous green waters of the Langebaan Lagoon. I had to take some form of action. Since I had work commitments which prevented me from going down to Marseille right then and there, we could at least catch up on the phone while we were in the same country.

From: Viktor   Tuesday, June 17 2008 8:24 AM

Hey,

Was great to chat last night - I have decided that your book is about your sexcapades, so I really want to read it now.
Am I right? Sounds like a great premise... or maybe I am being too bold :)

Viktor

We'd chatted for over an hour. His seductive accent made me melt. Through our conversation, I learned that he was actually living back in Canada where he was working for an international company with projects in France; how convenient! He was also living in Vancouver. Yet another coincidence. I'd always thought if I would ever move back home, I would go there. It was a vibrant, cosmopolitan city located in the most stunning setting, it had a bearable, mild climate (unlike the rest of the country). Plus my mother now lived in the nearby city of Victoria, on Vancouver island.

In addition to other general news about my current situation, I told him about the beginnings of my first book, which by that time, I'd been working on for around six months. I wouldn't have really qualified the subject as 'sexcapades,' as he'd guessed. Sure, that was one way to put the romantic disasters which I'd found myself embroiled in. I was hopeful that there was a cure for the curse Aphrodite, the

Goddess of love, had cast on me. Could it be Viktor? September didn't seem so far away. Even though I knew I couldn't get too excited (Viktor lived across the world after all), I was still quite keen on the prospect. If anything, his return reminded me there were other fish in the sea. Even if sweet Lionel seemed like Mr. Perfect, he wasn't necessarily 'perfect' for me.

A GOOD VINTAGE?

VINCENT [07/16/08 6:45 PM]
Why don't you stop by the shop?
Bring your friends!

OH MAN. My head hurts.

I couldn't bear to open my eyes. From the dim light creeping through the cracks of my lids, I could tell it was at least the morning, possibly even the afternoon.

What had we gotten up to last night? Or rather what *hadn't* we gotten up to? Vague flashes of memory came to mind as I agonizingly attempted to kick-start my brain. Drinks with friends at my place… A round of shots before leaving… were those roadies in the plastic cups we were holding as we made our way down to the Pigalle Rock Party? More shots… then some dancing… with boys?

"Zzzzzzz…"

Yikes! What was that? A snore? My previous reluctance to open my eyes disappeared as I heard a mysterious sound. I dared to peer out of my right eye only to find the blurry shape of another body in my bed.

Who was that?!

Before complete panic set in, a look under the covers concluded that I was mainly clothed as was the unknown snorer. Now that I was scared into wakefulness, I put the covers over my head and went back to piecing together our night.

Our super fun friend Cindy was in town, which inevitably meant we'd get up to a certain amount of mischief. I missed Cindy terribly. She'd been an important member of our crew before sadly moving back to Canada, taking with her a strapping young French guy, Cam, who'd started out as a casual rebound from her long term ex-fiancé. Now two years, later they were still together. He'd come back to France for his Masters and she was in town visiting him. I was secretly plotting to get her to move back as well—showing her a great night out on the town was part of the plan.

We'd gathered a small gang of our mutual buddies at my place for some munchies and warm up drinks. Before we knew it, Cindy was stoking the fires of our *petite fête*. As long as she had her way, the night would not be ending with nibbles and wine at my apartment. Just like in the 'old days,' she literally forced us into our dancing shoes and out we clip-clopped to the nearby Le Centre de l'Univers. A small historic club, it was turning into our favorite spot to spend our Saturday nights; no more O'Hooligans for us! Somewhere between a round of shots we really didn't need and the closing of the bar, the boy in my bed must have danced in my direction.

Luckily, I'd had enough brain capacity left at five in the morning when we stumbled out of the club to only loan him one side of the bed... to sleep. Cindy and Cam were camped out on the living room sofa bed, which had likely inhibited my unplanned house guest from trying to occupy more than his allotted portion of the bed.

Memory now more or less intact, I courageously braved a few more glances at the heavily breathing boy. He was actually pretty cute. He had short, dirty blond hair and appeared to be approximately my age. He'd also been out dancing at one of our favorite spots, leading me to believe he must have a fun spirit. I couldn't have imagined Lionel dancing till dawn with us.

My ponderings were interrupted by evidence of stirring in the living room so I woke up the sleeping *garçon* and we shyly slinked out into the living room, I wasn't even sure if Cindy would remember we had yet another house guest.

'Lunchner' was a tradition with Cindy, Cam and I. Since they didn't have their own place in Paris, and since whenever they slept over at mine we'd inevitably have late nights out, we never got around to having our Sunday hangover meal until 2:00/3:00 pm, too late to be considered brunch, so we nicknamed it 'lunchner.' Very serious brunch-style meals, each time we tried to out-do the last; taking turns to whip up the likes of scrambled eggs oozing with melty comté cheese or asparagus omelets sprinkled in fresh herbs, main courses accompanied by sweet potato fries or homemade baby potato hash browns. Regardless of the menu, it was always Cam's duty to go acquire a fresh baguette at my *boulangerie*—an unimaginable task for us two girls on these rough Sundays. On this particular one, it was my turn to prepare our feast, so I left Mr. Snorer to chitchat with Cindy and Cam while I chopped away. This was convenient, as I'd forgotten anything he might have told me about himself the night before.

Vincent—as we discovered was his name—seemed quite at ease amongst us strangers and was a good contributor to our casual over-easy conversation. Friendly, charming, cute, even excellent English... hmmm, not a bad start.

"So what do you do, Vincent?" Cindy helpfully enquired.

"Oh, I've just come back to France from Chicago where I worked for a wine importer for five years," he answered. So that's how he spoke such fantastic English. Living abroad also gave him some additional points: he was adventurous, brave and open-minded. In addition, he obviously knew a lot about my favorite beverage, granting him many additional points. My heart was glowing as brightly as a glass of rich, oaky white Bordeaux.

"Why did you come back to France?" asked Cam.

"Because I decided to open up my own wine bar!" Wow, he'd just elevated his Parker rating into the 90s! Cindy even gave me an approving look from across the table. Before he left, I was the proud owner of his business card and an invitation to stop by his *cave à vins* later in the week. This all seemed too good to be true. Could I have stumbled upon the right romantic blend of *amour*?

VINCENT [07/10/08 6:45 PM]
Why don't you stop by the shop
tomorrow? Bring your friends!

I was still a little nervous. I barely knew Vincent, so I wouldn't be stopping by *without* bringing some friends. *Les filles* would serve as good protection, plus I could get their opinion on Vincent at the same time. Besides, it wasn't like it was going to be too difficult to convince them to join me to drink what would definitely be excellent wine.

NAUGHTY [07/16/08 7:02 PM]
I'm in! It's only fair that we get to
meet him too.Cindy doesn't even
live here and she already has!

PUSSYCAT [07/16/08 7:04 PM]
Just around the corner from my
house? Score! Do you think he
has a loyalty points card?

THE COUNTESS [07/16/08 7:07 PM]
Will he give us a discount on our
Domaine de Valentin?

Located not far from Notre Dame and the Latin Quarter, Vincent was hoping to attract both locals and meandering tourists to his *cave*. However, the street was just a couple of blocks too far from the main tourist zone of the area; if any tourists did end up there, they would really have to be quite lost. At least those who did wander in could console themselves with a nice glass of wine served by a friendly English speaking *caviste*.

"*Bonsoir!* So nice to see you," Vincent greeted us four girls with his smoother-than-a-1980-Bordeaux accent. Setting us up at a nice table, he explained how things worked. His place was both a wine shop and bar with around eight tables. According to the particular business license he had, in order to be able to serve alcohol, clients also had to purchase some food. To this end, he produced a small menu featuring various *fromage* and *charcuterie* plates, plus a few daily specials. Since it was a warm day, we ordered a bottle of chilled Chablis and an assortment of cheese to go with it. Vincent popped by to add to our discussion whenever he could slip away from his other seated clients and the sporadic passers-by ducking in to pick up a bottle to bring back home for their dinners. He'd only been open for around a month, but it seemed like he was already building a faithful clientèle of neighborhood residents.

Once we finished the Chablis, Vincent didn't want us to go and, being the salesman he was, deftly convinced us to have a second bottle. It wasn't too hard to twist our wine-loving arms; this time we opted for a Sancerre—despite his encouragement towards a more expensive Burgundy. We did like our wine, but we didn't have the wallet to match the best *bouteilles*.

As it was a weekday and we all had to work in the morning, our two bottles didn't spill over into three, though he might have been able to persuade us to stay a little longer with a complementary glass of cognac, like he just offered to clients at another table. Never mind. We weren't looking for a wild night. Vincent bade us all a kind farewell, mine a little fairer, accompanied by a wish to see me again soon. So far, so good!

> VINCENT [07/19/08 3:15 PM]
> Salut ma belle. Are you free for a
> picnic on Sunday afternoon?

What a nice idea! Just the fact he'd suggested one of my favorite Paris activities made me like him even more. When Sunday rolled around I put together some tasty snacks and other picnic supplies, figuring these could go nicely with a bottle of wine from Vincent's shop. All packed up with my blanket and bottle opener, I jumped on the *métro* towards the rendezvous point he'd selected: the Parc de la Villette.

A contemporary park built around the Science Center and the Villette Exhibition Hall, I normally came out here during the August open-air cinema festival, like the fated time I'd met the mischievous Dutch-Canadian Mario. It wasn't the most picturesque green-space in the city, but it was home to vast lawns bordered by shady trees. Was Vincent missing large, well-manicured American parks? The inviting smell of fresh cut grass? This was certainly a rarity in the dense urban jungle of Paris.

Blanket lain, I began setting out the goodies I'd carefully prepared. At the end, I smiled, expecting him to produce a bottle of wine, some chocolates... fruit... cheese... *anything?*

Apparently he'd just brought... himself.

Hmmpf! It had been his idea to have a picnic; he hadn't suggested a simple walk in the park. Oh well, it wasn't the end of the world. Thankfully I'd packed enough food and, at the last minute, thrown in a bottle of water.

We gabbed away getting to know each other as we picked at our veggies, quiche and nuts. Then we sprawled out for a little rest. It was nice to cuddle and have some affection, that was... until he started pinching my arms. There was nothing affectionate or sensual whatsoever about that. Gentle caresses were welcome, but nipping at my un-muscular biceps was not! The worst part was he wouldn't stop even after I'd asked him to several times.

"Maybe it's time for a walk?" I suggested, trying not to sound too annoyed, as I proceeded to gather up the scattered Tupperware containers.

Thankfully, the little stroll passed without any unwanted flab fondling, and eventually the sun was disappearing behind the trees. This left us with a slightly awkward 'what do we do now?' moment. It was 7:00 pm. We weren't really hungry due to our afternoon of snacking, but it seemed too soon to end our time together just then. However, I wasn't about to invite him over to my place either.

"We could go grab *apéro*?" I suggested. Settling in at a café and then perhaps finding a place for a light dinner afterwards made sense. I could see him mentally hemming and hawing.

"Well, I need to watch my spending right now, with all the expenses of opening the bar."

"I know some cheap Indian restaurants not far away?" I proposed. I didn't need to go anywhere fancy; it was more a matter of spending more time together. Technically, since I'd brought all of the picnic supplies, it would have only been fair—in addition to plain gentlemanly—for him to offer me at least a drink. He continued to mull over the options while we walked away from the park and down the Canal de l'Ourcq.

Soon we reached the stretch along this wide waterway that had lively bars on converted *péniche* barges. They were calling us! Or maybe they were only calling out to me, as I could tell their pleas fell on Vincent's deaf ears. Even though I was a tad disappointed, ending our afternoon date there would be fine—it was nice to take things slow. Therefore, I didn't repeat my suggestion to go somewhere else when we made it to the end of the canal and were standing across from the *métro*. He gave me a passionate farewell kiss and off we went in our opposite directions. At the end of the evening, I was still left with a positive opinion of him; it was nice to spend some time together considering how busy he must be, and he'd eked out some time for me on his only day off.

Throughout the following week, I did receive a few sweet text messages from him and, as the weekend was quickly approaching, the girls and I were working out our Friday and Saturday night plans. Vincent was eager to have us stop by his wine bar again. However, with its meager menu choices, the girls and I compromised with dinner elsewhere in the area, and stopping by his place for drinks afterwards.

"He seemed very happy to see you!" whispered Naughty after Vincent had delivered our requested bottle of Côtes-du-Rhône to our table.

"I do have to approve of his vast knowledge of wine," added The Countess.

"Though, he's always recommending all the expensive bottles," Pussycat rightly grumbled. She knew her wines extremely well and we kept telling her she should become a sommelier in addition to her photography work, and eventually, maybe—thanks to one of The Countesses bonuses—we could all take early retirement on a vineyard in the South of France... *maybe?*

"Even though we'd like to drink Champagne or Châteauneuf-du-Pape every day, a crémant or a Côtes-du-Rhône would suffice for now," I noted, taking a sip of our very satisfyingly delicious blend.

"So you're willing to settle on a lesser wine... I hope your relationship standards haven't also slipped," said Naughty, using this as the opportunity to bring the conversation back to the reason why we were at this particular wine bar.

"Well, even the best wines need to age," I replied.

"Does that mean you're actually going to give this more than two dates?" questioned Naughty.

"It's sort of hard to decide what's been a date and what hasn't…" My beating around the bush sent the girls' eyes rolling. "Come on, girls! It's too soon to tell if he's actually a good vintage or not, but I'm willing to give him more of a try."

With that, Pussycat topped our glasses up and we had a celebratory cheers.

Our Côtes-du-Rhône was flowing as rapidly as the river of the wine's namesake, and after a second bottle, it was time to leave to catch the *métro*. This time it was decided: I wasn't going home alone.

"*Digestif*? Tea?" I proposed when we got back to my place. Vincent hadn't offered to bring any wine from the bar, so I was going on what was available in my meager pantry. We had a small glass of cognac and chatted for a bit on the sofa before he made a move. At the park we'd innocently kissed (and we most likely did that night we met), but that had been the extent of any 'action' up to this moment.

He put his arm around me as he leaned in for a kiss and I went to mirror his actions. It might have even been the first time I'd put my arm around him… and my hand stopped dead in its tracks as it rounded his shoulder. Wait a second, what kind of shirt was he wearing? It looked like a regular dress shirt. It may have *appeared* normal, but it felt… padded.

That was absurd—we were in the middle of summer. Something was wrong. Nonetheless, soon after we gravitated to the bedroom, but now with some trepidation on my part.

Eventually our clothes started inching off. It was dark, but the removal of his shirt confirmed the inkling I'd had from touching the back of his shirt just moments before... and it was just about one of my worst dating nightmares.

There's one body 'pet peeve' I have with men that is non-negotiable: back hair. Chest hair or a few light hairs on the shoulders or lower back are acceptable... but 'bear' level body hair—especially on the back—was completely out of the question. He was blond, albeit dark blond, so how could he be so hairy?

"Back in the U.S. I used to have it waxed. Maybe, I should start doing it again?" he actually admitted, obviously aware it could be a turn off.

What's this maybe *all about? Why had he stopped?* It's true, I have noticed in general, the French are less concerned about body hair and waxing, but nevertheless, this was extreme—I had an overrun vineyard on my hands! I couldn't believe we'd been joking earlier about owning a vineyard; I wasn't ready to do any pruning... certainly not on the *vigneron* himself! I just couldn't stomach it. I must have feigned fatigue or he might actually have been tired from his long week (or sensed my instant repulsion), but nothing much more happened in the bedroom that night. Although, sleeping on it wouldn't make the issue go away.

Before you ask why I didn't make an appointment for him myself at the waxing salon, other doubts about the quality of his vintage were slashing all of those Parker points he'd previously acquired.

Just like when he wouldn't stop pinching my arms in the park, the next morning as we were getting up, he began showing other odd ways of displaying affection: after more little pinches here and there, and playing with my underarms… I asked him to stop and instead he kept on going! *Hmmpf!* No, there wasn't any hair there… being the furry man he was, did he find that strange? I'm not really sure if anyone would find this very romantic, but I personally found it terribly annoying. The third factor holding me back from putting the boyfriend 'label' on Vincent would fully play out on the night before I went away on holiday.

We'd entered August, the traditional month for holidays in France. While the city's population didn't quite liquidate as much as it had in decades past, most of my friends had already trickled out of the city, leaving me on my lonesome for the week prior to my own departure to Canada on holiday. It looked like I'd be going by Vincent's bar on the night before my flight *toute seule*. This was perhaps not such a bad thing, as we wouldn't be seeing each other for a few weeks, and it would be enough time for me to reflect on the situation. Chatting a bit tonight would help me decide whether to bother with him not.

"*Salut, ma belle!*" He sweetly greeted with a kiss. He set me up at a table in the corner and I agreed to his recommendation a glass of crisp white Pouilly Fumé from the

Loire Valley. By now I knew this would inevitably come with some cheese. One glass turned into two as I worked away on my cheese plate, with his help when he'd stop by in between serving other clients. It wasn't very busy that night, so he was spending quite a bit of time at my table.

With the *fromage* finished, and the other clients paying up and on their way out, I thought we might actually get to go out for dinner and have some focused quality time together. But just as he was about to close up at 9:00 pm, a couple of regulars popped their heads in the doorway:

"*Vous êtes toujours ouvert?*"

No! My mind was shouting.

Vincent's chances with me weren't going to stay very '*ouvert*' if he was going to stay open for these clients. While I knew he had to please his growing clientèle, I did think it was a shame we wouldn't be able to have a proper date where I could mentally conduct an analysis of our situation.

Vincent set these new customers up with a bottle of wine and plate of cheese. I thought the least he could do was offer me a glass of wine to entice me to stay a little longer. Instead, he recommended a dessert. Not having much of a sweet tooth, I declined.

"I might even give it to you on the house!" he added, trying to sweeten the deal. What was this *might* all about? I really didn't want it, so if he insisted on forcing it upon me, I hoped he would offer it to me for free.

I smiled and changed the subject. Eventually, it came back around to that darn dessert, which was turning into as serious a curse as grapevine disease is to wine-makers. Despite my protests, a piece of thick chocolate cake suddenly appeared in front of me. *Really?* I was getting a little sick and tired, but it wasn't from eating the rich cake. I poked at it sparingly with my fork, while Vincent nibbled away every time he came over to my table. Since it looked like I'd been obliged to stay longer, I ordered a third glass of wine hoping it might help improve my mood; to no avail.

More clients came in, leaving me a few moments alone with my thoughts. I was becoming more and more doubtful I could be the expert vintner required to turn this blend into something worthwhile. My grape varietals seemed to consist of a hairy back, annoying displays of affection, severe frugality AND an inability to listen. It was like trying to make decent wine with a mix of Shiraz, Zinfandel, Chardonnay *and* Sauvignon Blanc grapes. This was definitely not a great combination!

For the time being, I tried to sweep those thoughts under the carpet—or rather into my suitcase. I might as well revisit them during my trip to Canada. The only decision I made right then was to finish up my glass and head back to my place.

"Don't leave yet!" Vincent pleaded, seeing that I was starting to gather up my things, he'd immediately whooshed over to slosh some wine into my glass from the bottle he'd just served to the other clients. This compelled me to stay a little longer, sipping slowly away at the small refill as Vincent chitchatted with his new customers. It didn't take me long to finish this new splash of wine and when Vincent freed himself from the other table, I asked him to help me select two bottles of wine for my brother who shared my love of *bon vin*.

"This Saint Emilion is wonderful," was the first suggestion to come to his lips. I looked down at the price. *Yikes!* I loved my brother, but I was thinking around ten to twelve Euro mark, not thirty and above! Was he trying to get me to buy the most expensive bottle in his shop? I managed to get him down a few notches on the price range and we settled on a more reasonable Côtes-du-Rhône, which the girls and I had had previously, and a bottle of reliable Languedoc, from the Southwest of France. He then tallied up my bill.

"I guess I'll leave off the cake and that little top up I put in your glass just now," he calculated. *Was he for real?* I hadn't even wanted the cake and that sprinkle of wine could barely even be considered a half glass. How could someone be so cheap! I certainly wasn't expecting the bottles of wine for free, however, I thought he might have given me an itsy-bitsy discount. I could have picked some up at my neighborhood wine shop for a good deal less and would have had the freedom to choose without *très cher* recommendations hanging over me. And, to boot, not even *one* of the real glasses of wine I'd had that evening were either free or discounted.

"Are you sure you don't want to stay a little longer?" *Why? So I can pay for more expensive glasses of wine, then take a thrifty, pinching, hairy beast back to my place? Non merci!*

"Sorry, I have to get up early to finish packing," I said, packing any chances of ever seeing him again into an empty magnum of Pomerol to be tossed into the Seine! There would be no need for 'further reflection' while I was on holiday. In all honesty, it might have been better this way. I'd be going back to Canada a free woman where—with any luck—I may even tend to those surprising romantic vines, which had been replanted by Viktor back in June.

My holiday voyage would be taking place in two parts. The first would take me to see family and friends in my native province of Ontario (including the delivery of that pricey wine to my brother) and the second leg would take me all the way out to the West Coast, where I'd be visiting my mother in Victoria and then my dear friend Princess Jess in Vancouver. Admittedly, I was also hoping to have a reunion with Viktor while I was there. So, as I was leaving for Toronto, I dropped him a line to give him the dates I'd be in town.

From: Viktor   Sunday, August 10 2008 12:33 PM

Hey Lily,

It looks like I will be traveling for work then to Germany and France. Let me know when you are on your way back through. I am sorry to miss you - it truly would have been great to see you. Stay in touch.
Oh - and thanks for the thong.

Sincerely, Viktor

No, I hadn't sent him a thong in the mail in a lipstick-sealed envelope! This was back in the early days of Facebook when everyone was 'poking,' or throwing random chatter at each other. My choice of a virtual thong might have been a touch provocative! But back to the real essence of his message. *He would be out of town? AND in FRANCE?* How could that be possible? We were swapping countries. Missing each other through revolving airport doors? Woe was romantically me.

> From: Viktor   Saturday, August 30 2008 10:47 PM
> Subject: getting into trouble?
>
> Hey there,
> How was Vancouver pretty lady? Did you get into any trouble? Marseille is wonderful, but would be better if you were here...
> Viktor

This was the message I received turning on my phone, as my recently landed plane taxied to the terminal at Charles de Gaulle airport. *How could Vancouver have been good when you weren't there, Viktor?* Getting into trouble? With WHOM? And now he was taunting me with 'wonderful Marseille'? I jammed my phone back into my pocket and groggily marched off the plane in search of my luggage carousel.

As soon as I got home, in the jet-lagged sleep deprived mind, I flipped open my computer and went directly to the French train company's website. I typed 'Marseille' into the destination box. The prices weren't extortionate. Sure, I was just getting back from holiday, but the weekend wasn't too far off. I really was prepared to drop everything and slip down to the Southwest to see him for a few days. I couldn't very well surprise him though, as I had no idea where he was staying and Marseille wasn't exactly small. So, I sent him a quick email suggesting my spontaneous plan, hit send, and then hit my bed, dreaming of waking up a few days later next to Viktor.

From: Viktor   Tuesday, September 2 2008
8:12 PM

Too bad - I am back in Vancouver now. I may be back in France next Spring, so perhaps we can plan ahead for then. Sad to miss you.
Xoxo V

Back in Vancouver? Already?? I was tempted to crack open a bottle of Châteauneuf (that was close enough to Marseille) to help drown my sorrows when I received a text message:

VINCENT [09/02/08 8:20 PM]
Hello my belle! Back from your
trip yet? I'd love to see you!

Uggh. Vincent. What to do with him? I knew where I could find that nice bottle of extremely expensive sorrow-drowning Châteauneuf, but I would not be going across town to Vincent's shop to get it. I didn't care if I hadn't seen Viktor when I was back home, and so what if he wasn't going to be back in France until—hypothetically—next spring? I would definitely not be seeking comfort in Vincent's furry arms. Could I just not reply to his text message? Would he get the hint and assume I must have fallen in love with someone back in Canada and had decided not to return to France… which had actually partially been on my trip agenda?

VINCENT [09/06/08 2:35 PM]
Tu me fais la tete?
Are you mad at me?

I received another message a few days later. 'Mad' wasn't exactly the right adjective. Fed up was closer. I was so bad at breaking up with guys and had a nasty track record to prove it. However, it looked like my usual horrible tactic of 'ghosting' wasn't going to work on Vincent. That same night was Naughty's birthday party, which she was holding at her tiny flat with a small crew of friends, so I sought out some much needed advice from the girls on how to handle the situation.

"Ghosting is terrible anyway," scolded Naughty.

"Oh, really?" I rebutted. "The other suggestions you've put forth in the past ranged from pretending I was pregnant to fibbing that I'd contracted a rare, contagious skin disease… Is flat out lying that much better?"

"What's ghosting?" asked The Countess innocently. The things she missed out on by not being on Facebook!

"Ghosting… as in disappearing like a ghost. It's when you don't write the person back," clarified the all-knowing Pussycat.

As awful as it was, it usually did work. I thought back to poor sweet Lionel, whom I'd sort of ghosted on, but not completely (I'd pretended to be busy twice and he went away on some work trips and didn't try again). He definitely deserved better than that. I wasn't sure if Vincent did, what with his unsavory behavior towards me. Although, it didn't really seem like I had a choice; he obviously was going to stick around like the aftertaste of a cheap wine. As they were bickering over situations when ghosting might be moderately acceptable, my phone started buzzing.

"Ah! It's Vincent!" I exclaimed. His ears must have been ringing.

"Answer it and pass me the phone!" offered Pussycat shrewdly. She'd have no problem telling him where to go.

"I've got the pregnancy story ready!" chimed in Naughty, reaching for the phone. I fought my phone out of their hands and let it go to the answering machine. We waited a minute and the phone started ringing, this time it was my answering machine calling back.

Listening to his message I could tell that he'd had been drinking and was rather exasperated about not hearing back from me. My response would call for a pro. We beckoned over our French friend Jeannette. She always managed to wrap guys around her finger; surely she'd be adept at flinging them off.

With her astute 'local' advice, we crafted a simple message explaining I was no longer interested, left out any mention of him being a hairy cheapskate with clam claws, and ended it with '*bon continuation*,' in French for coldly wishing him the best of luck. Hopefully he'd at least make it to the waxing salon before he met the next girl and, with any of the luck we'd sent him, she'd be the thick-skinned daughter of a wealthy wine baron.

Emotionally exhausted, I could content myself with being alone for a little while and would dream of next spring which could hopefully blossom brightly with Viktor's next visit to France.

BURSTING BUBBLES

From: Mario B. Tuesday, December 30 2008 12:28 AM
Subject: NYE

Ciao bella,

I am just back now... let me know how many of you are coming tomorrow and I need to talk to you about the drinks etc.. talk to you tomorrow or if you are free to come by???

Ciao, Mario B.

"DES BULLES! I want to drink champagne every day!"

Times hadn't changed, only budgets. Over the years, a range of my pals from my university semester abroad to Paris had done a pilgrimage back to the City of Light. This time around it was Donatella Spumante. She'd been my roommate and partner in crime to much Paris partying, with a third gal, Katia, rounding out our trouble-seeking trio. During those three months, which totaled ninety-one days, no more than ten went without popping open a bottle (or several) of our favorite discount sparkling wine. Within days of arriving at La Maison de l'Argentine (a cheaper option than our country's residence and one with cuter boys!), My new roomie and I discovered that: a) we both like to have fun; and b) that Paris was an expensive city. We'd have to be creative in order to achieve the former, with the latter obstacle. We succeeded, through some trial and error, eventually finding that a certain brand of *vin mousseux*—a sparkling wine costing less than two Euros a bottle—was the least awful of the bargain basement wines from the supermarket we experimented with. The bubbles most certainly helped mask its sub-par quality.

Now, almost a decade later, Donatella was married to the boy she'd started dating right upon our return from Paris (at least the aura of City of Love had worked on her), and had since become a high-flying corporate lawyer. The couple was over for a week-long visit, during which time we'd be having at least a daily bottle of bubbles and, as she pledged on the day of their arrival, among these *bulles* would be no cheapo *vin mousseux*.

"*Cheers!*"

Over the course of the next days we sipped on the finest French champagne, even better than the Domaine de Valentin I usually had with the girls, while catching up on the last few years of our lives and taking trips down memory lane to our exciting time in Paris, which inevitably led me to moving back permanently. I can honestly say it was the *best* time of my life. By day I spent hours wandering the halls of the city's top museums, and by night we were getting into some form of mischief, which took us to parties at the various residences of the Cité Internationale where we lived, dancing on tables at our favorite Dutch bar and a few random adventures, which weren't to be repeated in front of Donatella's now husband. One night during their stay, we even tried to go back to some of our old hangouts; however, finding most of them didn't serve champagne, we were forced to seek out the sparkling liquid gold in new places.

MLLE SECRET [09/27/2008 4:08 PM]
Whatcha up to tonight? Want
to check out this new
champagne bar with me?

What perfect timing! As a travel writer, Mademoiselle Sécret always knew the best places to go. This new bar, La Coupe, only served champagne. Not surprisingly considering its specialty, it was located in the chic yet sleepy 17th arrondissement, not far from the Arc de Triomphe and the Champs Elysées. The district's streets may have been lined with beautiful Haussmann-style Parisian apartment blocks, however, despite its glamor, it wasn't one of my favorite quarters of the city; though, on this particular night, some divine bubbles would make it dazzle. After a couple of text messages back and forth with Mademoiselle Sécret, we had that day's champagne quota lined up.

Entering the dimly-lit, tiny ground floor of the bar, sexy Mademoiselle Sécret was nowhere in sight, so we climbed up the narrow stairs to the second floor where we found a larger lounge area and the pretty Mademoiselle laughing away with an attractive stranger. *Ohhhh la la! Who was **he**?*

"Hey Lily, meet Mario." *Dio mio, another Mario?* I couldn't escape them. Unlike the unfaithful Dutch-Canadian Mario, this one looked like an authentic Italian one: tall and tanned with lovely chiseled features. Luckily, I hadn't had any champagne yet, or else I might have fallen right into his lap instead of my designated seat across from his beautiful *faccio*. He was straight out of an Italian romance novel and my mind was racing through its pages.

In no time at all, Donatella ordered up a bottle of Veuve Cliquot. Mario was extremely friendly and immediately launched into how and why he'd come to Paris. He was actually Italo-Canadian: both his parents where Italian, but he'd been raised in Montréal—unfortunately a similar story to the *bad* Mario—though I couldn't very well hold a grudge against all Marios from that creative, cool (in more ways than one) city.

With the cork popped and our glasses filled, he enthusiastically carried on with his story, which took him from Montréal to Rome where he'd worked for the U.N. *Ahhh...* my weakness for U.N. boys went faster to my head than the champagne bubbles. He'd recently taken a sabbatical to fulfill a lifelong dream of opening up a bar in Paris. Sexy, smart... and future bar owner? He seemed too good to be true! We laughed, chatted and sipped away at our champagne. By the end of the evening, he'd promised to let us know when his bar would be opening, in about a month's time.

"I organize events for a Canadian group, so let me know when the bar is open and I'd be happy to arrange a get-together there to help spread the word," I offered. It was the perfect excuse to see him again, and I wasn't even making it up! My past role as event coordinator for the Canadian Club had recently been recreated as the coordinator for the 'professional group' of the Canadian Women's Association. Like outgrowing the cheap wine of our youth, I was also moving up and away from my former days at the Canadian pub to what sounded like a sophisticated cocktail lounge.

"Lilace!" hollered Donatella when we left the bar. Oh boy, she hadn't used her old nickname for me yet.

"What?" I innocently replied.

"No hiding your admiration of that Italian Stallion," she noted. I couldn't get anything past her, plus she was probably right! I wasn't always shy with my flirtations.

"I was just being… friendly."

"Some things never change," she said. "And thank goodness for that!"

We'd gotten up to a good deal of flirting during our international exchange years before. An international campus meant lots of dreamy international boys. It hadn't taken Donatella very long to meet and hook up with the cute Italian who lived across the hall from us and Katia had a love triangle going with a Spaniard and a Brit. I, on the other hand, had a few of my own romantic misadventures, which could fill a novella.

"So where are you taking us tomorrow?" asked Donatella, in an overly bubbly tone.

I was starting to get a little champagned out… and craving Italian shaken cocktails.

Mario and I had exchanged email addresses, and now I had to play the waiting game. I'd been too busy gazing into his gorgeous eyes to ask him when the grand opening would be. Was it in a month or six weeks' time? Even with my handy excuse of the Canadian ladies events, I really didn't want to reach out to him first; that would make me come across as too keen. However, with no word from him by the end of October, I was getting a little antsy. The passing time was like an opened bottle of champagne: it was quickly fizzling out.

At the time, I was signed up for all kinds of Meetup groups, from Vegan Paris to Yoga in the Park. I practically never attended any of the events for which I received almost daily email notifications. This wasn't because they didn't sound interesting, but now having lived in Paris for so many years, it got tiresome introducing myself and explaining what had brought me here time and time again (a slight downside of living abroad, it's true). That said, I often skimmed over the email notifications to see what the events were about, in case I'd be tempted to go. It was on an early November morning I received a Meetup message entitled 'Italian Aperativo.' I couldn't help clicking in to see what it was.

The event was being held at a new bar opened by an Italian… which I guessed could only be Mario. Now that I had the name of the bar, with a little poking around online I'd found other references to it which seemed to indicate that it had actually been open now for a few weeks. *Hmpf!* While I was a little peeved that he hadn't let me know, I realized that he'd probably been so busy with the launch that he couldn't keep up with everything. I could understand that letting a fellow Canadian (that he'd met briefly) know about the opening was probably not at the forefront of his mind. Since I'd now acquired the bar's address, it wouldn't hurt to stop by and say hello, would it? I didn't want to go alone, but who else might be game for a little soirée of espionage?

"Another bar owner? Seriously, Lily," sighed Naughty.

"It's a pure coincidence, really!"

"Have you already forgotten about the last one?" questioned Pussycat cynically.

It was a toasty autumn evening and we were over at The Countess' enjoying some delicious, reasonably priced Minevois wine, well, particularly cheap for Naughty, Pussycat and I since we'd raided it from her Highnesses small makeshift wine cellar consisting of a few lovely wooden wine crates tucked under the staircase up to the second floor of her loft. She'd stocked up while down in that particular region the past summer where her parents had a vacation home in a small village near the historic and beautiful town of Carcassonne. We'd tried to stow away in her suitcase, without much success. There was always next year, but in the meantime we'd journey to this pretty part of France through its delicious wine.

"A cocktail bar, huh?" cross-examined the Countess, weighing up his worth.

"Vincent was different… he was a cheap furry bear!" I defended. "His flaws had nothing to do with his occupation."

This provoked raised eyebrows from the bunch of them.

"Besides, Mario isn't just a bartender. Don't forget: he worked at the U.N.," I added, assuming that would win them over.

"What about that bad British Brad who also worked for the U.N.?" reminded Naughty. "What good did he bring you?"

Uggh.

Brad, my devilish boy 'twin' whom I used to see off and on in my early days of living in Paris, well, 'off and on' because he wouldn't call me back for months on end. Both fun-loving and fun-seeking Leos, I was the more lovable one and he did nothing but seek fun, girls, late nights and excuses for showing up to work at noon. It was usually he who would leave me in the romantic lurch, however, the coin was flipped a few years back when he witnessed the most adorable Keanu Reeves type trying to hook up with me at the one of Brad's favorite haunts, effectively ending that vicious dating circle.

"That was U.N.E.S.C.O., okay, still the U.N., but Brad barely ever went to work anyway, it could hardly count as a job for him," I attempted to slide that old story back under the dating carpet where it belonged. "So no one wants to come with me? How about if I buy the first round?"

"Do you think they will have any champagne cocktails on the menu?" asked The Countess. *Yikes!* This was looking like it could get expensive. I was starting to regret the bait I'd used to try to get them to come. "Where is it, anyway?"

"Ummm, well, over by l'Arc de Triomphe, but it looks really near the *métro*." This triggered a wave of cringes amongst the girls. I too had cringed when I'd come across the address in the snooping around that I'd done. While not as bad as trekking out to the suburbs, it was right near the champagne bar Mario and I had originally met at; this was not only an area I rarely went to, but the girls were equally averse to it.

"I'm good to go along for a happy hour cocktail," said Pussycat—the bigger adventurer of the three others and with less expensive tastes. She'd probably be the best wing-woman for this particular mission. I didn't really trust either The Countess or Naughty to go with an open mind, and my Pantheon of Gods only knew what kinds of inappropriate comments Naughty might slip in to ensure I wouldn't be able to date another bartender or bar owner ever again.

Pussycat and I made a date for the following Thursday. The *aperitivo* event I'd seen had been held on a Wednesday, so I figured there were better chances there wouldn't be an event going on; thus, we could hopefully garner more of Mario's attention. In the end, there'd been no reason to worry at all. We were treated to all of it… because we were his only customers the whole night.

"Ciao bella!" Mario enthusiastically greeted us. He seemed genuinely happy to see us, not only because his bar was empty, but he was already having some woes. Commiserating about them would bring him some relief and I was more than happy to over him a sympathic ear… shoulder… lips?

"I thought since this spot was near the Champs Elysées we'd have all kinds of passers-by coming in," he bemoaned. Having never lived in Paris, Mario didn't know the city very well, and especially that particular area. While the bar's street was one of the main axes off *l'Etoile* (the insane roundabout encircling the Arc de Triomphe), the area was populated by offices, not evening-cocktail-drinking Parisians. As such, it was a virtual wasteland after 7:00 pm, albeit an elegant one.

"I can make you a flyer if you want? That way you can give it out to some of the offices or hotels around here," I offered. I'd already pledged to bring in my Canadian ladies, but helping him with a flyer would give me an excuse to come back even sooner. In fact, Pussycat and I were back the following week to take some photos and discuss the flyer details.

While I'd promised to make it, Mario was a little frantic to have it ready ASAP; within a week he was hurrying me to finish it. I put this down to his being stressed about opening the bar and the lack of customers. When I did send it to him a few days later, he wasn't entirely pleased with the results. *Sigh!* Beggars can't be choosers! First he rushes me, and then he isn't happy with a rushed job. Pussycat would have probably advised me to tell him to stick his flyer up his sexy Italian *derrière*. I didn't want to lose my only girl ally in my quest to conquer Mount Mario, so I just kept this itsy bitsy detail to myself. Besides my slightly ulterior motives, I understood his plight and I did genuinely want to help him. I made the changes he requested, however, his prickly attitude kept me away for about two weeks. When I eventually did go back in, with a visiting friend, Lizzy, he was back to his previous sweet, vibrant self.

"He seems really into you!" Lizzy whispered when he was making someone else's drink at the other end of the bar. Well, that was the frustrating part. While virtually every time I was at the bar, he'd squeeze into the conversation a somewhat flirtatious line such as 'pretty girls like you' and 'don't you look nice tonight,' his words never converted into actions. Would they ever?

From: Mario B.   Tuesday, December 30 2008 12:28 AM
Subject: NYE

Ciao bella,

I am just back now... let me know how many of you are coming tomorrow and I need to talk to you about the drinks etc.. talk to you tomorrow or if you are free to come by???

Ciao, Mario B.

It was now almost the end of the year. My normal Christmas trip to Milan would be shorter than usual this year as I was going to return for my first-ever Parisian New Year's Eve. Since it seemed like a good handful of my friends were also staying local, including Mademoiselle Sécret, the two of us pulled together everyone we could for a New Year's Eve party at Mario's bar. It was yet another attempt in what was an ever-growing list of efforts I was making to help him promote his bar. As he requested by email, I stopped by the night before to discuss the details.

"Geez, I hope it will be enough people. If I'm not going to make enough money, I'm not sure if it'll even be worth it seeing as I'll be working and not having fun."

"There will be enough, don't worry," I reassured him. "Plus, with all of us, it's bound to be fabulous!"

This didn't seem to console him much. This wasn't the first time I'd noticed his tendency towards pessimism. It was challenging to launch any new business; he'd be more likely to succeed by worrying less.

I didn't want our New Year's Eve to be a flop either! It had been his idea, but I had gone ahead with organizing it per his suggestion, and now I'd invited a bunch of people whom I'd assured would have a wonderful time. Of course deep down inside I was also hoping this would be a good way of bringing us closer together. If he was just a little more relaxed, maybe he'd actually put some moves on! Plus, it was one (or should be) of the most romantic nights of the year. To me, it seemed like the start of a new romance would pair so well with the start of a new year.

I had full faith that it would be a great evening, and it was. Mademoiselle Sécret and I had managed to fill the bar up nicely with happy revelers; Naughty and The Countess were away, but Pussycat was around and Cindy was in town, so she brought her boyfriend and his friends, which included Special Kay's beau therefore we'd be lucky to have her out with us as well. It felt like we had danced back into our former Saturday night routine. Mario eventually lightened up, possibly because he realized it would be a profitable night. Regardless of the reason, he'd was being exceptionally friendly to me. So as the party was wrapping up, I lingered around thinking that if we were almost alone he might make that move I was hoping for. However, he had nothing more to offer than a farewell kiss on each cheek. *What was I doing wrong?* Maybe it was the bar. I needed to get him out of there. The wheels in my head started turning, devising the perfect ploy… one which magically presented itself shortly thereafter.

A few weeks into January, Mademoiselle Sécret was having the official launch of her new book at one of the largest English bookstores in Paris. Even though I already had a copy of her book, I went to cheer her on while sipping a few glasses of free wine (always provided at these sorts of events to tempt in attendees). Plus, it was bound to bring out other expat friends we had in common, giving us all a chance to catch up after the holidays. In addition to these benefits of the evening, there was also a door prize. So after Mademoiselle Sécret gave us a reading from her book, we all quieted down as she drew the name of the raffle winner.

"Jenny Smith? … going once … going twice?" Since 'Jenny' didn't present herself, Mademoiselle Sécret drew another name.

"And the winner is… Lily!"

Wow! What luck! I went bouncing up to the front to accept my prize, which turned out to be two tickets to the Crazy Horse, the raciest of Parisian cabarets! I was instantly the best friend of all the men in the room, but I knew *exactly* who I was going to invite…

LILY LA TIGRESSE [01/17/2009 3:24 PM]
Are you free sometime next
week? I have a surprise.

I daringly texted Mario. I really had nothing to lose; this was my chance to get him out alone and to a sexy event to boot. One would think that this would encourage most normal guys to take some action, if they wanted to. I also knew his birthday was coming up, so it could certainly be packaged as an early birthday gift for him. He agreed on a date, and would leave the bar in the hands of his associate.

I still hadn't told him what we were doing, just to meet me at a designated time outside the *métro* near the cabaret.

When we arrived at our destination, he was indeed surprised to discover what our evening activity was. I'd explained how I'd won the tickets, we were served with a bottle of complimentary champagne, the lights dimmed and the stage curtains rose. Could they also rise on a sultry romance between Mario and I?

It was indeed quite the sexy show with scantily clad glamour girls doing various dance routines, though I'd been expecting it to be even racier. I was hoping we'd grab a bite, or at least another drink, in the area afterwards. However, Mario pulled out the 'I'm tired and have to work tomorrow' line. Defeated, I realized there would be no encore for tonight's show. On the remaining part of my solo *métro* journey home, to had to admit defeat. He obviously just wasn't into me. He was full of compliments and smiles for me, more than he seemed to give to other girls, but there was just something not right. I was ready to throw in the barmaid's towel, but this bottle of life bubbly wasn't empty quite yet…

ROXIE [01/26/2009 5:36 PM]
It's all set! See you guys
on Sat at 7:30 pm!

A few weeks back, as promised, I'd organized an after-work drinks event with the Canadian ladies at his bar. The night was going well: there were many possible new clients for Mario, including a vibrant, slightly older member, Roxie the artist. Over the course of our evening there, she could sense that I was keen on Mario and, in turn, took it upon herself to play matchmaker by inviting Mario and me over for dinner at her place. I'd now come to the conclusion that there was no match powerful enough to light Mario's flame for me. However, since we'd both already agreed to go, I couldn't very well back out. Instead, I brought along a gay friend of mine so it wouldn't seem like a double-date.

Roxie's apartment was one of the nicest of any of my Parisian friends. It was gorgeously decorated by artistic Roxie herself and had a gigantic terrace overlooking the city's skyline punctuated by the sparkling Eiffel Tower. The only catch was that it was a bit far from the center, in the residential suburb of Issy-les-Moulineaux, located just southwest of the Paris city limits. It was in zone two and accessible by the subway, thus it was a suburb I could handle going to.

As I knew the way there, the boys and I met up at the *métro* and we strolled over to Roxie's together.

We were enjoying excellent food and succulent wine; our lively dinner was going very well until Roxie embarrassingly started giving me compliments. Sure enough, she had matchmaking on her agenda. I could feel my cheeks started to flush.

"Doesn't Lily look so nice in that dress..." started Roxie. "Her figure is just so... so..."

"In Italian we could say *ciccone*," Mario suggested when she couldn't come up the adjective she was searching for.

"Ciccone?!" I winced in horror. My slang Italian was quite good and I had just been called... 'chubby.' While I wasn't rake-thin, and could stand to lose ten to fifteen pounds, I wouldn't have classified myself as chubby. I'm pretty sure Roxie had been searching for a term with a positive connotation, like sensual or voluptuous. He tried to backpedal, saying it was more of a term of endearment. Okay, Mario's parents were born in Italy, but he'd been raised in the very English Little Italy of Montréal. He'd picked up his Italian when he moved to Rome, perhaps he'd misunderstood what it meant? Or maybe *ciccone* is a cute expression in Rome? But in Milan, where I'd learned my Italian, it definitely leans on the side of fat. Is that what he thought of me? Is that why he didn't like me? Because I wasn't skinny enough for his liking? I wouldn't want to be with someone who didn't appreciate me as a person above all else, which didn't seem to be the case with Mario. I was defeated, not deflated of course, since he thought I was 'fat.'

"You're not fat," consoled The Countess. "Not that there would be anything wrong with being *ciccione*. Here, have some more calorie-free wine."

"I brought the calorie-free chips!" said Pussycat tossing a bag of Doritos on the coffee table.

"Men!" growled Naughty, cracking open our bottle.

February, with its continual grey, rainy skies, was not the best time to go on a diet. Instead, I turned to my trusted friends and our old trusted red friend le Saint Amour.

"Thanks guys! Here's to good friends… and returning back to wine," I said. "I could take a break from the bubbles and from Mario's cocktails. They were getting pricey anyway!"

"Full of sugar, too. He should have a few calorie-reduced options if he's so concerned about weight," suggested Pussycat.

"And cut back on the pasta portions for his *aperativos*," admonished The Countess.

"Ahhh, you guys are so… sweet?" I concluded, causing a fit of giggles to explode in the room and our glasses to be topped up by Pussycat. There was no way I could feel down with these great gals at my side.

That was it. I was done! I'd wasted five months pining over him. I could finally fully admit that he didn't like me; I would just have to put his incessant flirting down to his vague Italianness. The girls were kind enough not to rub it in my face; the signs had been there, I just hadn't wanted to see them. It didn't mean we couldn't be friends, but I'd try to avoid going by his place for a little while so I could mend my wounded heart. Instead I sought out drinks elsewhere.

"Too curvy?!" said Dave astonished. It was like I'd just told him wine was no longer served at Le Rendez-vous des Amis. "I'd say not curvy enough!"

It was good to see my old friend Dave and to be back at our old hangout. I hadn't been to the dingy dive bar we used to frequent a few times per month in ages. After trying to flirt with me—unsuccessfully—for several years, Dave had gone grazing in what he thought would be more receptive, rounder pastures: an African dating website. He'd precisely chosen that site with care, hoping to find a bounty of voluptuous, sensual women (exactly the kind he adored).

"Don't Italians liked Sophia Loren-types who ate a lot of pasta?" puzzled Dave. Like the girls, Dave's good nature and quirky sense of humor would provide me with a good distraction from Mario.

"Enough about bad Italian boys; how are things going with your beautiful African babes?"

"Well, there are almost too many, but there's always something wrong… one lived in the suburbs, one didn't shave, one was flirtatious yet nothing ever happened…"

Geez, it sounded like he was running into the female version of the *garçons* who'd crossed my path!

"Then I was waiting for the bus the other day and there was this terribly attractive Cameroonian lady waiting there too. We got to chatting and I invited her out for a coffee. We've got a coffee date for tomorrow," he continued, pleased with these new prospects.

"That's great news, Dave!" It was good to see another example of how fate can throw romantic candidates our way when we're least expecting them. Although that didn't guarantee they would be perfect matches.

"To voluptuous encounters!" He raised his glass in a toast.

I wished him good luck, something I genuinely meant. Plus, if he was dating someone, we could go back to hanging out occasionally without him trying to put the moves on. Our chat put one more shovel-load of dirt over the romantic grave I'd dumped Mario into.

It was February 14th. Valentine's Day. I couldn't bear to spend the evening alone, but there was absolutely no way I'd be making an appearance at Mario's. Luckily Pussycat was free and we'd made plans to be each other's Valentine with a not-so-romantic dinner together. At the end of the afternoon before going out, I spent some time catching up on emails. I'd already agreed to organize another Canadian after-work event at Mario's bar and I sent him a reply to confirm the date. A few minutes later my phone started ringing.

"Ciao bella!" cheered the voice on the other end.

"Oh, hi Mario," I replied less than enthusiastically. With my saddened heart, I wasn't really in the mood for casual small talk with him, especially today of all days.

"I just thought it would be easier to confirm the details of the *aperativo* over the phone," he said and launched into the date, the time, number of people, etc. Then he said, "Oh, and Happy Valentine's Day by the way..." and from there he went into a clumsy rant over how he can't focus on more than one thing at a time, he was so overwhelmed with the bar and trying to get it off the ground that he couldn't think about 'anything else.'

This was an apology of sorts, which made me feel at least not completely moronic for having persisted all of these months. Geez, men really can't multitask. It wasn't like I would have prevented him from making his bar succeed; on the contrary, I was doing everything in my power to help! I let him ramble on and we ended with a "See you at the next event."

I really was ready to move on, however, some sadness was still lingering, along with a distant glimmer of hope he might be more 'mentally available' in a few months when his business was firmly established.

The date of our Canadian ladies event quickly rolled around and, with a few weeks having passed, I was looking forward to seeing him the next day. That was until I received a message from him asking me to call back urgently.

He'd had another request to book his whole bar for a private event the same night as ours. Our group's event was not RSVP, so I had absolutely no idea who was coming and no way of contacting any possible attendees. When I explained this to him, he got upset and said this other group was going to be eighty people and he couldn't possibly turn down the money. In essence, he was kicking us out, but the worst of it was that he didn't seem to care. After all the hard work I'd done helping him with his events, and giving him ideas on new ways to promote his bar, we were being pushed aside: out of his bar and completely out of his heart.

He did apologize afterwards, but I didn't hold any more events at his place. This was definitely the big sign that even if he did become interested, he truly wasn't worth my while, as The Countess had intuited. Working for fancy international organizations didn't guarantee that one was automatically a person of dateable merit (I should have learned this lesson from my experience with bad Brad!).

Now spring was once again right around the corner, perhaps my error had been in seeking out romance in late autumn and winter? I was hoping to yield a better amorous crop in the coming months. It seemed that some seeds require more time before the seedlings break through the ground, and there was one rare African plant I'd been tending to, watering with care for months and months. Weeding seemed to be where I needed some work. I'd just gotten rid of a gigantic Italian weed... so now would this special *Viktorius* flourish this spring? Didn't he say that he should be coming over again for work soon?

> From: Viktor   Sunday, March 22 2009 10:37 PM
>
> Hey Lily,
> Thanks for your message. I'd hope to see you soon as well, but sadly travel has been cut to a min at the moment. I will keep you posted, but best wishes in the meantime.
>
> Viktor

Romantic woe was entirely me. Should I just go find a snowy cave to hibernate in and wake up next year.

TEEING OFF FOR SOME
POETRY GOLF

WALT [04/06/09 7:36 PM]
Lily, where have you
gone from my life?

OKAY, AS IT TURNED out, I didn't completely hole myself up in a cave. However, my 'puppy-dogging after someone who didn't like me' days were over. Who was waiting to pick up the lead?

It's hard to admit when someone doesn't like you. It's actually difficult to face, and so it's completely normal to be in denial and make excuses in order to save face. I was learning to accept the signs, and I'd have to go through a few more of these scenarios again, but the frustrating thing with

Mario was his mixed messages. We can't change others and we can't make anyone love us. A wise friend told me once, years later and in reference to someone else, love should be easy, and if it's a struggle (especially at the beginning), then it probably isn't meant to be. I'd come around to a similar line of thinking after the Mario scenario and so it was with delight that I received Walt's warm message. It appears that *someone* wanted me in his life! But was *he* the right person to have in *mine*?

Walt and I had worked together when I'd taught English at a university in a faraway Parisian suburb, not as far away as Malmaison where I'd met Lionel, however, much further than where Roxie lived, yet it was still accessible by subway. I had two separate groups: one on Saturday mornings, which was the big day with around a dozen classes; and the other on Monday and Thursday evenings, when there were only four groups. The evening teachers comprised of me, back then the twenty-six year-old youngster of the team; Joe, a forty-something musician who'd never managed to get his music career off the ground; the sixty-something sleazy program director who used to hit on me; and lastly, Walt, a forty-something aspiring poet. Walt used to flirt with me as well, but unlike our director, he did it in a cute, non-intrusive way. His wife, kids... and age had warded off any desire in me to serve as his poetic muse.

Since I'd escaped the hassle of trekking out to those lessons a few years ago, Walt and I had been in touch only on a few occasions by email. We hadn't seen each other again until he invited me to his poetry reading last year. It couldn't hurt to go; I could support his creative endeavors and catch up on his latest news. I hadn't really expected just how big his news would actually be…

I showed up a bit earlier than the advertised starting time of the reading, with the hopes of chatting with Walt beforehand (so I could also slip out discreetly before the end if the reading was putting me to sleep). It was being held in the basement of a Scottish pub on the fringes of the Latin Quarter, a few blocks from the legendary Shakespeare & Co. bookshop which had fostered the career of many a young writer for almost a century, as well as the Canadian Bookshop, which would eventually help foster mine. It seemed that this pub was making its own contributions to the literary community, or perhaps just promoting its alcoholism.

Descending the narrow stone stairs to the basement of the pub, I spotted the tall redheaded poet instantly. He greeted me with two big smooches on the cheek and, with glass of crappy pub-quality red wine in hand, he turned the first verbal page of this new chapter in his life.

Back when we'd taught together, Walt used to bemoan his French wife and how she didn't understand his bohemian cravings. Recently his marriage had ended, and now that his children were teens, he fought for and had gained his *liberté*. His free spirit had been supressed for over fifteen years, and it was time to unleash it. This sounded all fine and dandy; the complexities of each couple can only be understood by the two people involved, so I didn't make any assumptions or judge either of them. However, I wasn't sure if immediately moving in with a youngish, feisty German named Hilda had been such a *gut* idea, which is what he had done a few months previously, before the ink had even dried on his freshly-signed divorce papers. He seemed happy and, as such, I was genuinely happy for him. He'd returned to writing and was once again living the bohemian life he'd been yearning for. While this was mostly positive for him, it sounded like he was trying to make up for lost time, but he'd gotten more than he'd bargained for.

I didn't have a problem with the German artsy *liebling* he was dating, nor with his writing poetry all day and night, or even wine-filled poetry readings; it was how he was financing this that was problematic in my eyes. In between readings, Walt revealed he and Hilda had obtained a 'good' lead on a large stash of pot, and they were acting as the temporary middlemen for a dealer, a job that could potentially earn them upwards of 10,000 Euros. It all sounded like shady dealings, but since it didn't affect me at all, I might have said 'be careful,' and that was it.

After the reading, I didn't hear from Walt for months. That is, until I included him on the invite to an art show I was participating in and garnered this reply from him.

From: Walt C.   Thursday, March 12 2009 1:41 AM
Subject: RE: ART SHOW 2009

Lily,

I am in New Zealand and wish I could just get beamed up like Scotty and get the heck over there to see you.

Yeah the trip is fine and I will probably stay longer here in the south rather than Indonesia. Back in Paris in April honey, hopefully without any ties binding me from getting to know you sweetly, if you are up to it.

Hilda was rather jealous of you when she saw you at the poetry reading... now I am rather detached from everybody, except my story with the Russian who stole from me...

Do well in your show, and be in contact please.
Walt

When I asked him for more details, he explained that an unsavory Russian 'friend' of Hilda's had stolen their pot stash, leaving Walt in the lurch with the drug dealer—and God knows who else on his tail. He'd decided to flee while the dust settled by doing a bit of a tour around the world. My goodness! He really *was* making up for a lot of lost time.

From: Walt C.   Saturday, March 14 2009 2:15 AM
Subject: RE: RE: ART SHOW 2009

Lily,
You are so sweet. Is this art exhibition over now?
Hilda, well, it is rather hard with her. She needs to understand a few things that she never will understand, I think. About independence. She wants a sugar daddy and I am afraid I am not the one for that.

I know, for many women sugar daddies are fine, but I grew up thinking women could take care of themselves and not need such pampering, as if their vaginas were so valuable! Okay, they are! But the value of good love is better. It goes beyond sex, and that is where I would rather be: in love and with lots of good lovin'.

Is everything so calculating chez les femmes? Cuz Lily
dear I would love to get to you... Okay, I will go for a walk
on the beach.

Walt

Poor Walt! It was a shame to see him become so jaded, but it did seem like he'd rushed into things with Hilda at lightning speed. And while it must have been exciting, he'd probably been too mesmerized by her charms to see some of the warning signs. He was definitely not sugar daddy material. I can't imagine Hilda had ever thought that either. But I was sure of one thing: it would be great to be 'in love with lots of good lovin'... though was Walt really the best candidate?

WALT [04/06/09 7:36 PM]
Lily, where have you
gone from my life?

Walt wrote to me soon after his return to France and I was rather pleased to get a message from him suggesting we meet up; whether it would lead to any lovin' was still questionable. There was certainly no question that he was a smart, interesting guy and now that I'd 'grown up' a bit since we'd first met six years ago, the fifteen-year age different didn't matter quite as much. He seemed truly interested in me, which would be a nice change from that wishy-washy Mario. Plus, I was on the lookout for someone with a bit of a creative bohemian flare, an homage to my roots. That said, there were limits, and Walt had absolutely surpassed those this last year.

His recently zany behavior was surely an act of rebellion after years of repression, right? Still, love sparks or not, it would be nice to see him and hear about his global adventures while on the run. We made a date for the next week at an authentic, yet not too romantic Italian restaurant in my neighborhood.

WALT [04/11/09 7:40 PM]
Sorry running a
little late, will explain.

It wasn't an average first date (or was it even a date at all?), so I didn't really care that Walt was running behind as I might have, had it been with anyone else. I ordered myself a glass of wine and, ten or fifteen minutes later, he huffed and puffed through the door.

He hadn't changed at all since last year, or frankly since I'd known him: he was still the slightly disheveled, quirky Utahan he'd always been. It was a Tuesday, so the restaurant wasn't too busy which allowed us the leisure and tranquility to catch up properly—that is, after he'd caught his breath. We ordered a bottle of Montepulciano, which we cracked into over a few basic pleasantries. As our food was arriving, I assumed he'd launch into a colorful tale of his trip around the world, hoping to escape the chilly spring we were having with images of secluded Indonesian beaches and rugged New Zealand mountains. Instead, as the waiter delivered our piping hot pasta, he dove straight into his current situation.

"I'm living in a tent," he announced in exasperation.

Quoi?! A TENT? In Paris? Like the homeless guys down by the Canal Saint Martin?

I almost choked on my linguine. That was about the last thing I'd been expecting to hear. Okay, so he hadn't fallen back into Hilda's greedy arms, nor into his ex-wife's possessive ones, but didn't he have any friends he could stay with? Had he been so enamored with his tent life in New Zealand that he'd decided to keep it going in Paris? They were not quite the same climates at this time of year!

He went on to explain he'd pitched his tent in a corner of a golf course in the suburban city he used to live in. He wanted to be close to his kids—I guess that explained why he hadn't set up camp down by the Canal with the other tenters—but would his kids really want to visit him at his new rustic abode? Would they spend their nights roasting marshmallows over the campfire? Not in the windy, rainy April in Ile-de-France, that was for sure. The dismal weather wasn't the only thing making his house of cards crumble; he'd started attracting attention from the local authorities. The golf season was about to open and the posh putters surely wouldn't want to share their greens with a homeless poet.

"I was actually late coming here because I was photocopying some paperwork at the office. I have a meeting with the Mayor tomorrow. I think I have a strong case and I'll be able to stay the summer."

He was really planning on staying… *the whole summer?* Wait, office? What office? The office of the Association of

Homeless Writers, Poets and Artists? France seems to have an association for everything, so I wouldn't have been surprised if that were the case. No, somehow he'd been taken back at one of the English schools he used to work for, which meant he was most likely earning a decent salary. He could afford to pay for a little studio apartment somewhere, or perhaps a simple, cheap hotel in his suburban town until he had enough paychecks to be able to rent a real place of his own. So, why didn't he?

Wow, this story really took the cake—or rather the tiramisu—that wrapped up the meal I ended up treating him to. This was fine though, he obviously needed to save all the money he could.

"A TENT?" howled Naughty, almost knocking over her glass of wine as she threw her arms up in disbelief.

"Was it one of those large multi-room ones?" asked Pussycat. "So he could have a bedroom for the kids? That might not be so bad."

Oh brother, I shouldn't have told the girls. I would never live this one down.

"I'd expect nothing less than a *château*, Lily," scolded The Countess.

"Sigh, you guys are totally right." I'd already resigned myself to the fact there was no way it could possibly work out with Walt. There was only so much bohemian-ness I could take; this was borderline insanity.

"On the bright side, you could have learned how to golf for free," suggested Pussycat. The other girls didn't find that funny in the slightest, fearing I might actually take a liking to the idea.

"Don't worry, girls," I said, hoping to prevent them from lynching both Pussycat and me. "Sure, I wanted to find someone who would really love me and someone interesting, but even I'm not *that* desperate."

"No more poets!" ordered Naughty.

"And be wary of tents," warned Pussycat. I didn't tell them my mom had lived in a teepee for a little while in her 'I'm not a hippy' days. That would have riled them up even more.

No, as much as I wanted someone bohemian and didn't need to date someone who was super rich, Walt's wacky situation and state of mind were just a little too 'off the wall' for me. Walt would have to write his poem for another muse and I would need to find my Prince Charming elsewhere. Maybe in Vancouver? What was that Viktor up to anyway! Sure, I let myself get distracted by these other oddball suitors (or snobs), but it had been practically a year since my adorable Namibian friend had re-entered my life, and as patient as I was trying to be, I was beginning to wonder if I should give up hope on him altogether. I was reminded there were other options out there and, as with Walt, maybe they would come to me instead of me chasing after them, like I had done with Mario and Viktor.

A KNIGHT IN SHINING ARMOR
WITH GOLDEN WINGS

AS PER MY USUAL, the quest for a happy medium somehow always got derailed—or like in the next stage of my romantic journey—drift from its flight path. Fasten your seat belts, put on your chainmail: a medieval-style turbulence zone lies ahead.

Over this last year I'd succeeded in whittling down my English teaching to only a few hours a week. These included a couple of private students whom I'd been teaching for years; classes on film terminology and usage at one of France's most prestigious film schools where I'd harbored a secret desire of getting hired on for a real job… that is, until I realized the slightly nightmarish conditions of working in any French bureaucratic institution: snail-like pace in getting anything done (but without the tasty garlic butter which made *escargots* palatable), more levels of hierarchy than a *mille-feuille* cake, tyrannical directors that would scare the Revolutionaries out of their graves); and lastly, a few extremely well-paid, in-company lessons for business executives. All of these were my direct clients, rather than through one of the shady English schools I'd previously worked for, which greedily kept most of the profits. As such, I was pocketing all the profits and, even after taxes, it was amounting to between forty and fifty Euros an hour, *pas mal du tout*. Regardless of the good paycheck at the end of the month, I was still dying to get out of teaching. Now, I was getting enough work tour-guiding and had been offered a new part-time consulting opportunity for the tour company, I'd decided to slowly cut my teaching ties by not renewing most of the teaching contracts as they expired.

An exception to this plan arose one day in early May, when I received a pleading email from the former Human Resources Director of the film school. He'd shifted back to the private sector and was working for a prominent French travel company. In his message he explained that one of its directors was in desperate need of some short-term classes.

Since it would only be a thirty-hour contract, I figured the time should go by quickly enough, and it would bolster my bank account ahead of the quickly-approaching summer holidays. In addition, as I was starting to get involved in the travel industry, I thought it could be a beneficial learning experience for me as well.

One slight downside was that the office was out in the suburbs, but at least it was in a nearby one, Issy. This was where Roxie lived and where I'd had that disappointing dinner with Mario in attendance. Oh well! I didn't harbor any negative feelings for the place, and in fact, it was on my regular *métro* line, so I wouldn't have to spend ages getting there.

On the day I was meant to go out to their office to meet my new student, give him a test to check his fluency level, and discuss the curriculum, I was running a touch late as usual (possibly a tendency I'd picked up from the French). When the last sheets of the test eked their way out of my printer, I scooped them all up and raced down to the *métro*. I had also printed out the address and a Google map. If I had difficulties finding their offices, I could ask a local for directions once I arrived down in the neighborhood.

Bounding up the *métro* steps in Issy five minutes shy of the scheduled time, I wiped the sweat off my brow and studied the map. Wait a sec, this didn't seem right. With no time to lose, I approached a group of men standing in front of the corner café who looked as if they'd grown up and never left a five block radius of the main square, they'd surely know the street. However, I was only met with bewildered looks. I didn't have time to waste as they scratched their heads trying to think of where it might be. I scurried into the café and showed the bartender the print-out of the email from the VIP's assistant.

"*Mademoiselle, cet adresse n'est pas à Issy, c'est à Ivry,*" he responded.

Crap. I'd gone to the wrong suburb! Seeing that it was short and started with the letter 'I' I was so used to coming down to Roxie's I hadn't even paid attention and was now in the *complete* opposite direction. Perhaps it was a sign I didn't really want to take on this new class?

I called up the director's secretary who said it wasn't a problem; he could see me anytime that morning, so back down the into the *métro* I raced. By the time I retraced my steps into the city, then zoomed down to the southeast and crisscrossed my way on foot through an industrial zone that seemed a world away from pretty Paris, I arrived almost two hours late in a hot, flustered mess.

I announced myself to the receptionist and attempted to regain my composure as I waited on a sofa in the bright, spacious lobby. A smiling middle-aged woman arrived, shook my hand, and escorted me up to the top floor. Down a long corridor, she opened the door to a large office. At the other end, a tall, dark-haired, refined man stood up from behind his desk to greet me.

"Hugues de Viellebride d'Aubusson," he said in the most eloquent, elegant accent, extending his hand in my sweaty direction.

Who? What? I was too stressed over my immense tardiness to even somewhat comprehend what he'd just said. Had it been his name or an incredibly formal French greeting? Both hypotheses were entirely possible. I slid sheepishly into the cushy chair across from him and made some polite small talk to gauge his level of English before producing the grammar test from my briefcase. That would hopefully occupy him for enough time for me to fully catch my breath.

"Is Jack: a) looking after, b) looking up, or c) looking... at a word in the dictionary?" he puzzled, raising his frustrated eyes to mine. Oh dear, thirty hours was absolutely not going to be enough. Mr. Unpronounceable-Named Sales Director, whom I assumed to be in his late thirties and educated at France's best private schools and universities, must have completed his studies before the French had started taking English seriously, and it appeared he'd managed to evade having to use English in a professional setting, until now. With globalization in full swing, he had no choice but to improve his terrible *anglais*.

I'd soon learn that he didn't like being told what to do and that he was used to always getting his way—or almost always. There was no magic 'on' button we could switch in our brains to be able to instantly speak another language perfectly, high-level 'Sales Director' or not. I abandoned the test, not wanting his ego to suffer too much damage. It was obvious we'd have our work cut out for us.

Despite his annoyance and embarrassment over his dismal language skills, he remained courteous and charming, though with a brusque, busy businessman edge. After twenty minutes his phone started buzzing, so we set our first official lesson for the following Thursday—at least now I knew how to get there—and I gave a big sigh of relief as I slithered out of this suburb and back to Paris as fast as I could.

The first language lesson for true beginners usually starts off with learning the words which complete a family tree. I would hardly have expected my first class with Hugues to follow this same theme, but it was far from the basic genealogy of mother, father, brother and sister.

It turned out that the long name he'd indeed introduced himself by, during our first meeting, dated back almost 1,000 years. With extreme pride—and a certain degree of linguistic simplicity—Hugues explained he came from a very important noble family from the region of Provence in the south of France. He was a count and beheld not just any old 'de' (well and he actually had two...). One of his great-times-fifty-grandfathers was a Grand Master of the Knights Hospitaller. A crusader! He'd been a real medieval knight in shining armor, and now his modern-day progeny was edging a little closer towards me, staring intently into my eyes.

This wasn't the first time I'd come face to face with high-brow nobility, something which we don't really come across much in North America, but which still exists in some European countries. I'd had a flirt with a posh, future Grimaldi count named Eduardo, of the same lineage as the royal family of Monaco, when I'd been on exchange to Italy at age seventeen. A fellow exchange student, Tara, had been paired with Eduardo and was living in their castle near Vincenzo. It was south of Milan, where I was living with a fabulous and completely normal *famiglia*. I would have never wanted to swap kingdoms with Tara, the young noble had already taken on regal airs and was a pain to live with. However, I did manage to swap a few kisses with the count-to-be when I took a chaperone-less weekend trip with them to Florence, a princely city with all its turrets and towers. Eduardo would eventually inherit his family's title when his uncle died; he only had daughters and the title could only be passed down to male heirs. I'd be long gone to other kingdoms by then.

Back in France, the days of revered French nobles during the crusades and the grande époque under Louis XIV eventually led to some rockier times for French aristocrats at the end of the 18th Century, to put it mildly. At the time of the first French Revolution in 1789, only about 1% of the population of France were true *noblesse ancienne*, those who'd sworn oaths of fealty and performed military service for the king in exchange for their titles, a tradition going back to the 14th Century. Hugues' family belonged to this distinguished minority. Many other aristocrats merely bought their titles or obtained them through royal favors. Considering that a great deal of heads belonging to a noble 'de' (as in de Viellebride d'Aubusson) were lost to the guillotine, Hugues was just plain lucky his lineage had survived at all, possibly a reason he was even prouder of his heritage.

During the 19th Century, noble rights were reinstated several times, but any special privileges Counts, Viscounts, Dukes and Princes once had under *l'ancienne régime* were stripped once and for all in 1870. They did manage to retain the right to any property that hadn't been pillaged during one of the country's four revolutions—if they could afford to maintain it—and the 'de' which had fallen out of fashion for fear of being lynched by revolutionaries, had eventually crept back into usage. The grand names and families of the past didn't mean much outside their elite circle; however, today most carrying a 'de' wore it proudly, with a decent degree of self-righteous arrogance. Right at that very moment this sense of privilege, of having whatever one wants, was being directed right at... me.

I looked away and blushed, but he did not. These would not be any old regular English lessons. It appeared I'd have to take up fencing lessons in my free time to be able to compete with Hugues' skillful parries. I could sense that he took deep and daring lunges towards his goals, but what were these exactly?

He was a modern-day knight in shining armor! It was straight out of a princess storybook. In addition to carrying down the family tradition through his name, in the first few lessons I learned that Hugues maintained a large range of other regal customs such as:

- Castles: He had a massive Parisian 'palace'-sized apartment facing the royal Luxembourg Gardens in addition to several country estates. I'm sure one of them must have turrets.

- A horse: All knights should have a horse, right? Hugues had several and one on which he played polo during weekends.

- A carriage: Well, he had the contemporary equivalent: a plane. He worked for a travel company after all, and could virtually jet wherever he wanted at the drop of a hat (or crown).

This all sounded perfect, right? There was just one, very substantial glitch in this fairytale plot: the title of *Countess* de Viellebride d'Aubusson was already taken and the lineage would be maintained by their three small junior Count and Countesses.

"A Count? Now we're talking. Although you'd have to give me a new nickname," joked The Countess. It was the first Sunday of the month, a day when all French National Museums were free. The forecast had predicted nice weather, so we'd planned an excursion and picnic to the Château de Versailles, all too fitting a setting for me to explain my latest romantic entanglement.

"What's higher in the ranks? A Countess or a Marquise?" she went on in her ponderings.

"Marquise. Then from there it goes up to Duchess, Princess, Archduchess and finally Queen," precised Pussycat. She ought to know; her last name had royal connotations. "But it wasn't always so advantageous to be higher up."

No, it definitely was not! whispered the ghost of Marie Antoinette as we strolled by the little Norman village she'd had built so she could occasionally get away from court life. She could certainly get away from the court for a while, but she couldn't escape the court of the revolutionaries.

"Alright, fine, I guess I'll just have to become The Duchess then," she resigned, exaggerating her grievance with a flourish of her hand.

"Dukes, duchesses, marquises… Does any of that *really* matter?" said Naughty, gritting her teeth. "All that *counts* is that he's married!"

I could see that Naughty was fuming from us even joking about the possibility of ceding to any of his invitations.

"Didn't Louis XIV have five mistresses or something like that?" The Countess breezily pondered, innocent to the fact Naughty was firmly against cheating.

"Certainly even more than that!" calculated Pussycat.

"Isn't the French tradition of mistresses a bit… *passé?*" criticized Naughty. "We're in the 21st Century, for crying out loud!"

Naughty might have brought up a correct moral point; however, from personal experience, it didn't necessarily matter which century we were in. This was not the first time I'd met a count nor was it the first time I'd been the target of some serious flirting by a married student. The memories of the gallant Jean-Claude were all too fresh. He was an older student who pulled out all the (wrong) stops in his attempts to woo me during a private 'class trip' to Normandy. Afterwards I'd joked had he been younger and the owner of a private jet I might, just *might* have considered being his mistress. I should never forget that you have to be careful what you wish for.

"Don't worry, *mes princesses*. I have no intentions of becoming a royal courtesan," I said in an effort to diffuse Naughty's rage. I definitely do not condone cheating and I wouldn't actually have considered allowing him to achieve his conquest. That said, some French couples do seem to have this *laisser faire* attitude toward affairs and seem to put on 'what we don't know won't hurt us' blinders. This didn't necessarily pass in my books.

"Shall we go have a look at the stables?" I carried on with my attempts at diversion. "I hear the royal carriages are quite spectacular."

The stables seemed like neutral enough territory without too many references to extramarital mischief, though who knows what they'd get up to on those long bumpy journeys from castle to castle! And it looked like my journey through the rest of my lessons with *le comte* would be equally bumpy.

"Mauritius Island was *fabuleux*, I really think you would like it there. Or should I say 'fancy' it there?" His flirtations had started subtly, so much so that at first I wasn't sure if he was actually serious, but his invitations and compliments increased at the speed and ferocity of the final crusade to the holy land.

"Come in Egypt with me. We can do my class from there."

"It isn't come *in*, it's come *to*," I corrected, trying to turn the conversation back to grammar.

"But it would give us lots of time to practice useful vocabulary for my job," he continued. "Flying expressions, restaurant etiquette, hotel terminology. I don't even know words like *baignoire, oreillé... room serveece*."

"Well, the latter is already an English expression. You just need to work on the pronunciation," I highly doubted he truly needed to know how to say 'bathtub' and 'pillow' for professional purposes, and I didn't think exchanging pillow-talk was on the regular agenda at his business meetings! Egypt was high on my list of countries to visit; however, if I went with Hugues, I didn't think I'd be seeing anything beyond his luxury hotel room.

Hugues wasn't just a Count, he was also a persuasive and experienced 'salesman' and daring entrepreneur. Fresh out of business school, he'd started up his own travel company, which specialized in tropical island holidays. He went on to open a larger package holiday company. Its success soon attracted the attention of one the world's biggest travel companies, which bought it out for a hefty price tag.

Hugues not only got a good pay-off, he was also made Sales Director of its French subsidiary. Like a true crusader, he loved risks, and did whatever it took to win.

"Look at our new Tahitian bungalows. The bedroom overlooks the beautiful blue sea. Imagine waking up in this very large, comfortable, king-size bed to that view. So romantic... *n'est pas?*"

"Isn't it. The expression you want is 'isn't it,' " I mustered, trying to squeeze in some pedagogy.

Maybe it hadn't been such good a suggestion to practice for his upcoming presentation.

"Isn't it a pity we aren't in Tahiti right now? Is that correct, isn't it?" This was hopeless.

The flirtation meter rose in virtually every class; nevertheless, up to then it was mainly suggestive. Sure, he was definitely not suggesting I go to Tahiti with him to stay in the oh-so-romantic bungalow *next to* his. The French were quite skilled at flirting, and gentlemen of a certain class were often adept at suggesting a bedroom liaison without putting it in exact words. It was like the previous attempts made by my former student Jean-Claude. He'd never asked me if I'd be his mistress, but his passionate declaration of his adoration and other word-smithing clearly expressed his ardent desires.

As our class hours decreased, the dial of the flirt-a-meter skyrocketed until it was about to burst.

"I want to kiss you," he boldly proclaimed in the middle of one of our last classes, piercing me intensely with his eyes.

I was so caught off-guard, I was speechless and might have stammered something like, "Oh that's nice, now let's get back to this mergers and acquisitions vocabulary."

That proclamation made it official: I had a little bit of a dilemma on my hands.

Let's just imagine the best-case scenario. Sure, the prospects might seem very tempting: free trips around the world; staying in the most fabulous hotels and dining in Michelin-starred restaurants; weekends at a country estate in Normandy and summers at the family *château* in the South of France. Hugues wasn't even all that much older than me, and admittedly, he was rather attractive... but he was married. We hadn't really discussed the relationship he had with his wife, besides a few grumbling complaints about her nagging now and then. Even if they were on the cusp of getting divorced or lived separately (which was unlikely), an important fact remained.

He was a real Count. This family heritage weighed heavily on who he was, his lifestyle choices, and the circles he moved in. I was the furthest thing from nobility. I did grow up on a large property in the country, but our humble farm was no noble estate. It was like I was the milkmaid and he the master.

I was just downright too practical. I was well-educated, cultivated and classy, but I'd never fit in with the 'de's.' I couldn't wear a big hat and prance around at the races. I would be hopeless at hobnobbing and gossiping, while sipping Dom Perignon at ladies-who-lunch events with the other Countesses, Marquises and Duchesses; though I could do this very well while drinking our reasonably-priced

Domaine de Valentin with my own gang of pseudo-princesses. Our version of *la vie à la française* fulfilled my 'French dreams,' which were not missing the appearance of a traditional knight in shining armor. A contemporary one could be nice… a relationship could possibly work out with a young, cool Count, a black sheep-type who didn't give a damn about his 'de'! However, this was definitely not Hugues.

"Today, I am going to kiss you," he fervently declared. It was our last class and so he was making his last-ditch effort. Did he really like me, or was he merely so determined to succeed he wanted to at least partially achieve his goal to win me over?

"How about we go for dinner, then we could talk," I countered, finally responding to his advances.

All things considered, maybe there was something I didn't know about his situation? Since he'd been so adept at passing his message across without putting any intentions into words, and since I was trying to keep things professional and get through our lessons, it was a tad difficult for me to say *What would your wife think about that?* which could be a way of broaching the subject of his status with his *Madame la Comtesse*.

He seemed rather satisfied with my suggestion, and we set a date for the following week.

I was a tiny bit nervous. Of course this mightn't be such a good idea, but it would give us the right setting to be a little more upfront and natural. He might actually reveal he is indeed available (maybe his wife was leaving him for a Marquis?) and come across as less Count-y in a more relaxed context.

I didn't even have the time to think about what outfit would be worthy of this regal dinner or how to avoid being forced to eat fish in the surely classy restaurant he'd choose. The day before our scheduled dinner, I received a call from his secretary saying he have to cancel the 'appointment' he had with me because something had 'come up,' but that he'd be in touch to reschedule. It was probably true; with his high-pressure job, 'things' came up all the time. Or had my knight lost his courage? Had it all been a game of conquest for him?

I never heard back from the Count. It appeared he'd taken off his chainmail and sheathed his sword. Alas, there was no fairy-tale ending to this little fable. Hopefully another knight in shinier armor—one that was more compatible and single—would rescue me from my romantic doldrums.

From: Viktor   Monday, September 7 2009 11:54 PM
Subject: Labor Day weekend
Dear Lily,
I hope your summer has been epic. Just got back from camping on Prince's Beach. It reminded me of the coastline near Marseille. Here's a photo I thought you'd like. Can you spot me   in the distance?
Wish I could come this fall...
Viktor

I wish you could too, Viktor. Will you ever?

THE WILD BOAR WEARS PRADA

LUCA [11/19/2009 1:00 PM]
You absolutely HAVE to come for dinner,
come on! Otherwise we will never get to
see each other!! I await your news, but I
don't want to hear no.

WHAT DO A wild boar, fine dining, Russian vodka, and Hugo Boss have in common? I was about to find out!

"Cara Lily, next Monday you have plans. Reserve the night. Un bacio."

This was Giovanni's voicemail, received in mid September. *Hmmm...* What was he cooking up this time? It didn't sound like it would be one of the 'average' Italian feasts he regularly prepared for me, including the likes of soft rounds of burrata mozzarella, slices of perfectly grilled *zucchine* and copious plates of pasta draped in his various secret sauces. These meals were all served with the best reasonably priced French wines and capped off with a glass of succulent *grappa* he personally imported in from *Bella Italia*. I was always ready for some fun and surprises, and this one sounded particularly delicious.

I'd been introduced to Giovanni many years prior via another Italian, Roberto, a philosophy professor whom I had met during my semester abroad in Paris. Roberto had been doing post-post-post doc research (a forever academic) and wasn't one of the regular troublemakers I hung out with, though since I spoke Italian, we instantly hit it off, but only as friends. I was very fortunate he was still living here (working on yet another post doc) when I moved back a year and a half later. Not only was it nice to have a ready-made friend, he also gave me useful advice on finding my first apartment and helped me ease into 'real Parisian life,' which turned out to be slightly less rosy than the student bubble I'd grown accustomed to living in.

Since then, Roberto had taken a position at a Midwest American university and I could tell he was a little bit bored. Although he reassured me he was taking regular trips to New York, to take in some big city life (and possibly to meet some pretty, big city gals). Even though we didn't hang out much when he was living in Paris, he was one of my first friends in what would be a growing list of 'the ones who'd left'—one of the big downsides to life abroad. The girls and I had already bid tearful farewells to Cindy (well, she did reappear now and then), Lieutenant Steve, and his wife Nat, who used to be part of our gang and a few other friends. The rest of us were here to stay... *right?* My once adamant refusal to ever leave Paris was beginning to waver, after all. Perhaps it was the seven-year itch? If the right opportunity—or person—came up, I was leaning more and more towards moving on to a new locale, not necessarily back home, but perhaps somewhere else in Europe, like my beloved Italy.

But back to the Italian(s) in Paris!

One day I received a very rare email from Roberto asking if I might be interested in giving English lessons to a dear friend of his. Roberto's email ended with something like: *He needs them very badly and only for a short period of time.* This was when I was still teaching English regularly, so having another cash-in-hand student wasn't an undesirable prospect. So, I reached out to this friend, who turned out to be Giovanni.

"Come over for dinner and we can discuss," was the first of many Giovanni's dinner invitations. The English lessons never managed to get off the ground, but a cherished friendship did.

Giovanni was a sixty-something poet (Yes, another poet! However, I would not be enticed by the romantic allure of a poet; I'd learned my lesson from oddball Walt). Growing up in the Italian Lake District, his bourgeois background was dramatically altered when he moved to Milan for his studies in the politically tumultuous late 1960s. He became involved in an anarchist faction similar, but less violent, to the *Brigade Rosse*, and after he'd stuffed me with his delectable pasta dishes, he'd top up my *grappa* and add in a dose of lively tales of his risky exploits with his brigade. I was entranced by his stories about robbing banks, carrying out other misdemeanors, and flirting with as many girls as possible along the way. This behavior eventually led him to take exile in Mexico (I was always suspicious that it was more to do with his multiplying girl troubles rather than legal ones). Giovanni was definitely a ladies' man, but he never—or rarely—tried to cross that line with me, and we developed an uncle-niece-like friendship.

Even though he didn't have much money, and whatever capital he did have was from *never* paying his rent. He was a man of elegance, good taste and useful connections. I knew any invitation by him would be bound to lead to a fascinating evening. As such, after receiving his voicemail, I called Giovanni back to RSVP to his invitation. During our chat he offered up some additional information: a mysterious friend of his would be coming to Paris the following week. He explained that his friend had started this new tradition of taking Giovanni out for ritzy dinners whenever he was in town on business, expensing each of these *grandes soirées,* or rather, *grande serate*. This certainly appealed to Giovanni's low bank balance and high gastronomic standards. This time, his friend had told Giovanni to bring along a few guests.

Since I spoke Italian and am a lively conversationalist, I was a suitable candidate to call on. He'd also invited another Italian-speaking friend of his whom I'd never met: a graceful Chinese poetess.

The night of our dinner, I dug out an elegant enough little black dress, fixed myself up and made my way to the address in Giovanni's text message. He'd explained to me that our host loved this particular refined seafood restaurant near the Gare Saint Lazare, and insisted on always dining there at least once during his Paris stays. It was far from an ideal venue for a vegetarian, but Giovanni had called up the restaurant to check and they said they would pull something together for me. He'd assured me there would be nothing but the best wines, which would make up for my destined boring meal of vegetable side dishes, I was bound to be stuck with at such a traditional restaurant.

As I approached the large glass door of the classic old-school *brasserie*, it magically opened.

"*Bonsoir, madame*," the Maitre 'D said invitingly, impeccably dressed in a black suit and starched white shirt. Before I even had the chance to explain whom I was joining, boisterous laughter and loud Italian voices broke out deep in the restaurant, echoing throughout the whole dining room. My smile and nod of the head were met with a lapsed moment in his stoic professionalism, revealing his woeful anguish—it seemed like they were used to this southern guest's extremely non-Parisian behavior.

So who exactly was our extravagant host?

He was the stylish, mid-forties director of an important Italian textile company, which supplied fabric to some of the world's top fashion houses. He and his colleague Luca came to Paris a few times per year on business, usually during fashion week. The days were full of rushed meetings with designers and executives… and the nights were long, with an abundance of posh troublemaking.

"Champagne *per tutti!*" he blazed. The best bubbly in the house promptly filled our flutes, kicking off a vivacious night of overlapping discussions, hearty laughter and bottomless glasses. The champagne was followed by a Chablis Grand Cru to accompany their starters of smoked salmon, and my dismal salad of a few leaves of lettuce and couple of quarters of unripe tomatoes. A vintage white Châteauneuf-du-Pape accompanied their hundred and twenty euro lobster or perfectly grilled sea bass, and my selection of vegetable *accompagnements* (just as I'd predicted). With each refill the Italians got louder and louder, much to the dismay of the other diners and the staff, who were helpless to the expensive whims of our platinum card group. In one of his many unruly rants throughout the evening, the leader of the pack roared: "*Sono Il Cinghiale!*" or, *I'm the Wild Boar!* This repeated declaration was made all the more real with his mimicking of the ferocious forest animal digging its hoofs into imaginary dirt, grunting, preparing for attack. From this point on, our host's nickname became *Il Cinghiale*, or The Wild Boar, which seemed to match his over-the-top, predatory nature to a tee. Though, what was his prey... or rather, *who?*

Apparently Il Cinghiale had an insatiable appetite for lobster AND lovely women. Luckily, I was sitting next to Luca, a safe place well out of the Wild Boar's charging path. When the beast wasn't monopolizing the whole table's conversation, Luca and I had the chance to chat.

Also superbly well-dressed, he was a little younger than his gregarious boss, probably in his late thirties. He was friendly, yet on the quiet, modest side, and so was virtually the polar opposite of Il Cinghiale. In the moments when we could get in a smidgen of conversation amongst ourselves, I learned that he was the company's lead fabric designer. As such, he flew around the world consulting with their clients on designs for upcoming seasons, and then converting their wishes to fabric back at their factory in Northern Italy's textile region. How cool was that?

Hmmm... Was Luca himself equally cool? Or was his job the most impressive thing about him?

Dessert was served with a final glass: a small snifter of sensual plum liqueur. We'd closed down the restaurant. The poor, exhausted waiters were loitering patiently in the background, waiting to tidy up the mess created by Il Cinghiale's culinary rampage. I could almost read their silent prayers begging the heavens that The Wild Boar wouldn't return anytime soon, though now—after spending some time with charming Luca—I was hoping they would!

LUCA [09/24/2009 3:44 PM]
Dear Lily, how are you? I hope to
see you soon, maybe even next
month. A big hug, Luca

Ah ha! What a nice surprise! Luca must have asked Giovanni for my number. The riotous dinner might have unearthed something besides Il Cinghiale's pretend dirt.

LUCA [10/06/2009 7:59 PM]
Hello dear, I'm in Japan right now
but I hope to see you in Paris soon.
We'll stay in touch to organize
a nice dinner. Big kiss, Luca

I was soon getting a cute little message almost once a week from him… and from all over the world! While not postcards, Luca did make me think back to the sweet (but square) Lionel. Could Luca be the right combination of fascinating, cultivated *and* thoughtful?

LUCA [10/15/2009 6:08 PM]
Ciao Lily, Come stai? I'm on my
way back home from Germany. I might
be back in Paris by the end of the
month. Un bacio, Luca

"Could you get any free clothing samples next time?" questioned Pussycat.

"Valentino, Prada, Hugo Boss, Chanel… Now we're talking. Bravo, Lily!" enthused The Countess, proudly patting me on the shoulder.

"Soon that'll be you!" exclaimed Naughty, pointing to the window display in front of us.

We were having a lazy Sunday stroll. Our promenade which had started in the Tuileries Gardens, the setting of much prancing around during fashion week, had turned into an aimless meander through the nearby streets, leading us to the rue Saint Honoré, home to many of the most glamorous boutiques in the city. A dazzling gown had caught Naughty's eye in the Armani storefront window.

"Well, let's not get ahead of ourselves… but then again, it would be rude to refuse, obviously," I replied, eyeing up the dress, a truly gorgeous work of art.

I'd never been much of a fashionista, but I did aim to dress smartly and was usually found in black skirts and patterned tops or dresses. I didn't really follow trends and the only time I could be caught flipping through fashion magazines—whose pages were filled with anorexic models in clothing I could never afford and, even if I could, wouldn't fit me right—was at the dentist's office. Nevertheless, on this sunny autumn day, some window shopping and dreaming of possible dates with charming Italians was my hot runway ticket.

"And where did you say he just was? I can't keep track," asked Pussycat. "It seems you can check off the 'well-traveled' box on your list."

"And he most likely gets to travel first class," snuck in the luxury-minded Countess. "Maybe he'll invite you to tag along on his next trip?"

"Which would be fine... as long as *this* particular big traveler isn't married like the last one!" growled Naughty. I could almost see the smoke beginning to waft above her head at the mere thought of extra-marital affairs.

"No ring that I could see and no aristocratic '*di* - equaling big fancy Count' in his name," I quickly noted. The last thing we needed was to get Naughty started on one of her anti-cheating rampages; her growing fury might turn her into a wild boar herself!

"Plus, he most certainly has good taste in food if he's always dining in top-notch restaurants for work," noted The Countess, whose heart was often touched by sophisticated gastronomy.

"No roasting veggie dogs on a golf course campfire, which could have been your fate if you'd stuck with that homeless poet," tacked Pussycat, causing even Naughty's flames to be smothered by giggles.

"This is all much more promising indeed!" concluded The Countess. "It almost calls for a celebration... Actually, I just so happen to have a bottle of Valentin chilling back at my place..."

"Hot diggity dog!" chipped Pussycat. "Why didn't you mention that before? It's *apéro* time!" With that, we abandoned the unattainable attires of this swanky *quartier* and hopped on the subway over to The Countess's city castle garret, in search of a celebratory drink.

With all this talk of Luca, I couldn't help taking a step back from the situation and asking myself if I could start seeing him more seriously. I love Italy. Ever since I lived there for a semester in high school, the beautiful and culturally-rich country had occupied a very important place in my heart. I always knew I'd end up living there again one day; however, I figured it would be much further down my road of life. My hopefully-early retirement plan was to park myself at a restored, rustic Italian villa somewhere in Tuscany or along the Amalfi Coast, where I'd enjoy *la dolce vita* and entertain a steady rotation of visiting family and friends. Now with Luca in my sights, this idea started to become a bit more concrete and timely. Would I be ready to move to Italy sooner, if for the right reason?

At this stage in my life, I didn't think it was quite the moment to move to a countryside villa. During that semester I'd lived Milan, where I still have many close friends and my surrogate Italian family. While Rome might be a nicer city to live in as a young adult, because of my connections to the country's fashion capital, I could feel at home there… but that wasn't where Luca lived. He was stuck living in the small city of Biella, located in the heart of Northern Italy's textile region where his company's factory was. It was eighty kilometers from Milan and not easily accessible from Paris. I really wasn't sure if I could envision myself living in that dreary city. *Let's not get ahead of yourself, Tigresse…* Like I'd told the girls, I had to calm my imagination, as it had a tendency to carry me away. *Con calma.* We'd have to see how things went the next time I saw Luca.

"Il Cinghiale is coming to *townnn...*" sung Giovanni into my voicemail, like he was announcing the arrival of Santa Claus, which I guess he was, in a culinary sort of way! Ohhh... maybe I'd get some pretty fashion sample from this unusual Santa?

"He wants you to bring along a pretty friend," Giovanni added.

Ugghh. The invitation came with two problems. Firstly, I actually had a previous engagement on the night they were requesting our courteous presence. This I could try to move. I'd also received a nice message from Luca the same day letting me know about their arrival and I mentioned my scheduling conflict:

> LUCA [11/19/2009 1:00 PM]
> You absolutely HAVE to come for dinner,
> come on! Otherwise we will never get to
> see each other!! I await your news, but I
> don't want to hear no.

That was awfully sweet of him! I was pretty sure I could get out of the other commitment, but that left me with the second issue over The Wild Boar's special request. *Bring along a pretty friend?* Why? Was it just for dinner company... or to quench his thirst for fresh blood? I didn't run an escort service, but I did have some pretty friends who liked adventurous fine dining like me. Naughty was no longer as naughty as she used to be, and I was pretty sure she might spit venom at Il Cinghiale if he tried anything, and I was quite certain that, despite their fanciness, the Italian's noise volume might be too much for the refined Countess. So I went straight to my best bet.

"Sounds fun!" Pussycat eagerly agreed to go with me—I'd left out the specific request for pretty girls to avoid any reticence on her part. We'd surely be fine. Like her willingness to check out Mario's cocktail bar with me, I was in good hands with Pussycat. Plus, she was looking for the right 'big break' into fashion photography, and perhaps Il Cinghiale could help her professionally (hopefully without expecting anything in return!). I probably should have warned her that we were about to enter a forest with ferocious, dangerous beasts inside it, and she should come armed with her shield and sword.

> LUCA [11/24/2009 11:24 PM]
> Ciao Lily, how are you? Were you able to cancel your other engagement so you can come to dinner with us? I hope so!!
> A huge hug and have a nice day.

Luca definitely seemed keen to see me. I had to admit, I was really looking forward to seeing him, too.

The dinner went much like the previous one: rowdy chatter, lots of bubbly, fabulous wine and extravagant additions. I had my immaculately-pureed mashed potatoes and green beans drizzled in the finest Normandy farmer's butter—and the divine Châteauneuf-du-Pape was making up for the chef's inability to be creative in this old-school venue. I wasn't sitting next to Luca as Pussycat and I been the last to arrive; however, we did get to lean over to chat in between The Wild Boar's loud bursts and his competition with Giovanni over who had the most outrageous stories. Soon, he was taking us on an imaginary tour, with gestures to match, of his collection of sports cars, racing around the winding roads of the Alps in his Ferrari.

"*Andiamo a balare!*" shouted Il Cinghiale. He was all fueled up and raring to go. *Dancing? On a Monday night?* That was practically impossible in Paris, unless it was upon the tables of the student bar we used to go to when I was on exchange here. Somehow I didn't think that would be up to the Wild Boar's standards, though there would be plenty of pretty young prey for him to stalk. The best venue we could think of was the Guru Lounge, a vast, chic bar and restaurant near Place de la Concorde, and around the corner from all those posh boutiques on rue Saint Honoré.

Off we trotted, sent on our way by the cheerful *au revoirs* from the wait staff, barely able to contain their bliss from our earlier-than-closing-time departure. We piled into two taxis and quickly arrived at our destination. Even at the lounge, the atmosphere was rather subdued due to the boring night of the week, but at least it was still open. At this new venue I was sitting beside Luca, which gave us a proper chance to talk, well, at least whenever Il Cinghiale wasn't interrupting us with another exuberant *cheers!* … and another… and another. One, then two bottles of champagne turned into a deluxe bottle of Russian vodka. Unlike cheap mass consumer vodka, this premium drink had a sophisticated, smoky taste… almost foggy…

Yes, definitely *fogggyy*…

"*Svegliati…* Wake up, little Tigresse," whispered a soft voice. *Ouch!* My head felt like it had been trampled on by a herd of wild boars or a parade of stiletto-clad runway models. *Hey, wait a second!* Where had that soothing voice come from? I had this blurry intuition it might actually be a real one and not in my head. As real as the hand now caressing my arm… and the body curled up behind me!

My brain jolted to life and began desperately scanning my memory as to what might have happened the at the end of the night. All I could remember was the smoky vodka… which had obviously smoked over my memory AND better judgment!

I did a quick assessment of the murky situation. I was at least partially clothed, as was my bedmate… Considering the situation and the silkiness of the voice, it could belong to no one other than Luca. I must have been quite out of it and, instead of sending me alone in a taxi back to my place, Luca had taken me to his hotel in the Marais where we were now squished into one of the twin beds in his room.

He'd probably been hoping to get lucky; however, from what I sensed (and what Pussycat later helped piece together), I'd probably passed out in the taxi and he'd been gentlemanly enough not to take advantage of the situation. But now, early in the morning, he was stuck like glue to my body, as I was currently only in my underwear and bra. He must have also only been in his underwear and from what I could feel from what was against me... well... there wasn't exactly much to feel.

It was true that Luca was definitely a bit taller than me, but only by a couple of inches, and he was as skinny as those toothpick models he designed fabric for. The assumption that short, thin men aren't well endowed isn't always true, but it unfortunately seemed to be true for Luca. Not that I was about to let him remove his briefs to find out for 100% certain! When his hands started wandering a little lower than my arms, my mind and body miraculously jumped to action and began thwarting his cheeky advances. Sure, this might have been the perfect occasion for a few flames to spark, nevertheless, over the course of the night I'd started to wonder if I was actually really interested in him. Don't get me wrong; Luca's super slender 'physique' was not the only aspect that made me unsure about him as a serious candidate.

While he was a kind, elegant and intelligent person, he was constantly belittling himself and saying how things never worked out with the girls. This is not something to say to girl who you want to like you! Modesty is one thing; martyrdom is another. This, stitched together with the less-than-desirable prospects of becoming an Italian housewife in a depressing industrial city, and my hunch about his... equipment... did not come together as the beautiful, *haute couture* romantic design that I wanted for myself.

Luca had to get up for some early meetings, though I wasn't sure how he'd be able to function. I took my throbbing head back up to Montmartre and made a beeline straight for my happily empty, queen-sized bed.

PUSSYCAT [11/26/2009 10:35 AM]
Are you alive?? Il Cinghiale
tried to walk me home and we
almost rolled into the Seine!

I awoke a few hours later to this text message from poor Pussycat. *Oh no!* What had I gotten her into! That said, of all the gals, she could certainly handle her own. The Wild Boar had probably launched an attack, but he had a feisty adversary in Pussycat. I hoped she would eventually forgive me; and the invitation to fashion events, which proceeded to roll in from Il Cinghiale *probably* helped!

"But did you even like him?" asked Special Kay with a raised eyebrow. I didn't think the other gals would be all that thrilled with my wishy-washiness about Luca; it just so happened that a few evenings later I was having a rare one-on-one dinner with Kay, so I thought I'd get some advice from her. She was still completely smitten with her French *amoureux*, or should I say *fiancé*. After two years together and one year of cohabitation, he'd popped the question and she didn't hesitate with her *oui!* She was achieving her dream: marrying her perfect *français*. If she could succeed in finding true love, perhaps she could give me a few pointers, as I was proving utterly hopeless.

"Well, um, ah... maybe?" I stammered unconvincingly, biting into my veggie burger. While not a vegetarian, health-conscious Kay was generally eager to try out the new vegetarian places that were slowly opening up in the city. We weren't terribly impressed with the consistency of this particular 'burger'—it was holding together about as feebly as my feelings for Luca.

"Why do you give these guys a chance when it doesn't seem like you're actually all that into them?" This was one of the many questions Kay threw at me during our meal, which was slowly turning into the Spanish Inquisition. Kay had always been much more selective than me (well, besides her previous obsession with her boss' lame son; otherwise, she'd rarely given other guys a chance). Maybe her approach was indeed more successful. It was definitely food for thought I began to mentally chew on.

NEW YEAR, NEW BEGINNINGS?

ANTOINE [01/07/2010 3:13 PM]
Recherche: Charming company for a night
out in Paris. Are you free? I'm in town for a
few days and it would be marvellous to
see you. Bisous tendre, Antoine

AS WE NEARED the end of the year, what Special Kay had asked and the whole recent series of dating disasters were weighing heavily on my mind. Kay had a point. Whether it was warm-hearted Lionel, considerate Luca, or off-the-wall poet Walt or actually any of the others I chanced upon over the years, there were many to whom I'd given too much of a chance, despite not having intense sparks. On the other end of the spectrum, I'd also pined after two heartless Marios and other troublesome jerks.

Could I really be as picky as Kay? All the same, I couldn't bear the thought of being stuck in some Parisian suburb or a dreary middle-of-nowhere Italian town preparing dinner for my 2.01 kids as my businessman husband drove home from the office or from some business trip I wasn't invited to go along on. I'd simply go crazy.

Once again, I was finding myself drifting aimlessly along the same River of Dead-End Relationships. Well, maybe, they weren't even really relationships. I didn't even know what to call it at this point! The River of Disappointing Men?

There was actually a deeper reason, something that was constantly there, constantly lingering at the back of my mind when it came to romance: The Prophecy.

When I was sixteen and still living in the Canadian countryside, I had the opportunity to see a psychic, a friend of my aunt's. Now, we're not talking about some old gypsy with a scarf wrapped around her head peering into a crystal ball. She was a real, renowned medium. During our reading, she predicted I would end up living abroad, but also said I would meet my soul mate 'later on.' At that age, 'later on' really felt like a century away, (well, actually, it was since this was in the 1990s!). While I did fall for a number of guys in high school, university and afterwards, I always felt reluctance to let these early relationships evolve. I'd always step back and ask myself, "What about the prophecy?"

Achieving the first part of her prophecy started with studying abroad in Italy, and then in Paris, where I really did feel destined to live.

After a few years living in Paris, I was once again invited to visit a psychic; this time around, it was via one of my students, and the medium was actually a police officer who had certain esoteric gifts. These talents certainly must have come in handy when interrogating criminals... they didn't stand a chance lying to him! He knew all.

The crazy thing was, he'd said the exact same thing as the first fortune-teller: that I'd meet my soul mate 'later on.' He also included some very precise comments about my future amour, a repetition almost word for word as his predecessor, the words which would haunt all of my romantic decisions... and would come up 'later on.'

While this might come across as far-fetched and hokey, the fact that both prophesied the same destiny did leave an impression on me, and crept up whenever I ran into candidates whom I thought fit the profile they'd described. Was it finally 'later on'? Was *this* man the one? This questioning often got me into sticky situations, like giving cheating Mario too much of a chance. The reason I was stuck on this River of Disappointing Men was partially because I was waiting for this romanticized notion of 'later on,' but now, into my thirties and having gone through more than my fair share of distressing romantic trials and tribulations, I was more determined to shrug off the prophecy. I could design my own destiny! I had to try to take some control over the course of my love boat.

But first things first, I had to deal with my ship's stowaway: Viktor. I couldn't seem to kick him overboard just yet, however, I was sick of cruising around the same dating destinations time and time again.

Just then, the perfect opportunity to put on my captain's hat appeared in the form of a modern day telegram:

From: Facebook   Monday, December 21 2009 00:00
Subject: Facebook Friend Birthday Alert!

Viktor's birthday is in three days. <u>Send a Birthday Greeting Card</u> and make it a real special day for Viktor! <u>Click here for gift suggestions</u>!!

Hmmm... This email gave me the perfect premise to reach out to my stowaway, but I didn't need to send him a generic Facebook-formatted card! I could come up with my own creative birthday greeting.

It could have been the result of too much Domaine de Valentin with the girls in our pre-Christmas holiday drinks that night, or it could have just been the thought of Viktor's handsome face, but when I got home from The Countess' place, some naughtiness crept into my imagination. I took red lip liner and wrote *Happy Birthday Viktor!* above my cleavage, framed by a lacy red bra. I took a selfie and cropped it to be somewhat revealing, yet not too much and sent it off to Viktor with a satisfying smirk. Now, if that wasn't enough to get a reaction out of him, I didn't know what would!

From: Viktor   Wednesday, December 23 2009 11:51 PM
Subject: re: Bon anniversaire!

Made my day!
Xoxo

From: Viktor   Wednesday, December 23 2009 11:58 PM
Subject: re:re: Bon anniversaire!

And let's work out meeting up, however, March is too soon for me. How do I get to see more? :)

Ah ha! My special card *did* work! He seemed very keen to see more of me, but would he come to Paris to achieve this? I'd thrown the suggestion of a visit in spring into my original message, which was sadly deflated. North Americans didn't get as much holiday time as Europeans; however, couldn't he slip in a stopover in Paris on his next visit to see his family in Africa? Or couldn't he convince his job it was absolutely essential to reinstate those trips to France? Was there really any hope in waiting for him to perhaps come my way, or for our paths to intersect on my next trip back home? I didn't want to live in the suburbs or a small Italian city, but Vancouver was a much different and tempting story. Nevertheless, I would only consider moving back if I had a very good reason. How much longer could I really wait for Victor? Why wouldn't he just make a move? Even a tiny, virtual move would be a good start. Was it his distant but powerful grip on my heart strings that was keeping me back from meeting someone else instead of the prophecy? I was at a loss... For the time being, I'd leave the boys behind and bunker down in Milan for Christmas. Ten days of amazing food, great times with friends and the warm winter Italian sun were exactly what the love doctor called for as a remedy to my heartache.

LUCA [12/25/2009 12:57 PM]
Ciao Lily, my best wishes for Christmas and for a wonderful new year. I'll be in the mountains for NYE so I won't get to see you in Milan, but I hope to come to Paris soon. A big kiss, Luca

Okay, boys weren't completely off my mind during the holidays. Luca and I had exchanged a few text messages before Christmas; I thought if he was around and could come down to the real city from Biella, I could give him one more chance. Was his being away just a matter of fate telling me things were truly not meant to be? I gladly accepted his good wishes for the new year and put him away in a temporary drawer in my mind.

Perhaps my romantic situation could advance to a new page with the turning of the calendar?

ANTOINE [01/07/2010 3:13 PM]
Recherche: Charming company for a night out in Paris. Are you free? I'm in town for a few days and it would be marvelous to see you. Bisous tendre, Antoine

It looked like my odyssey was taking two steps back rather than forward one! I hadn't seen zany Antoine since that seductive afternoon in Montmartre with 'Adrien Brody' and his sidekick. Who might he have with him this time? I'd be more than happy if he was accompanied by, say, George Clooney or Ryan Gosling. George already had the villa in Italy so that would solve my villa issue and Ryan, well, we did share the same nationality and he was simply 1,000% dreamy.

ANTOINE [01/07/2010 4:05 PM]
Fabuleux! It's a date then! My friend Thomas and I are going to an African music concert in Belleville, shall we meet directly there?

Thomas, huh? Thomas, as in Tom, like Tom Cruise? Wasn't he a Scientologist? I didn't need a return of them into my life! Before my line of thought got too out of control, I decided it wouldn't be a terrible thing to see what this Tom was like. Meeting up with Antoine would at the very least lift up my spirits, which had definitely fallen a notch from returning to chilly Paris. I also welcomed any distraction from my recent romantic dilemmas.

The Belleville neighborhood, tucked away in the northeast of the city, was gradually becoming hip and gentrified, although it still hadn't shrugged off its working class roots. A walk through the cosmopolitan area could take you past a Chinese grocer, a Jewish bakery, an Arab shisha pipe lounge and an artist squat. Colorful as this might be, it was not exactly a place a single girl would want to walk through alone, particularly at night and veering off the main avenues and down its dark back streets. But here I was, meandering through the sketchy streets, slightly terrified and desperate to find my destination. I'd wanted a fresh start for the new year, but right at that moment I'd just be happy with making it through that day alive! *Au secours!* Help! The immediate question on my mind had been "Where is the love of my life?" but it very quickly became "Where the heck is this bar?"

"Bonsoir, ma petite Tigresse!" welcomed Antoine with his habitual enthusiasm. It was easy to forget about the darkness of my journey here with the sunshine Antoine emitted.

"This is Thomas," introduced Antoine with an extravagant wave of his arm, a flourish only a game show host (and

Antoine) could pull off. Alas, sitting across from Antoine was no George or Ryan look-alike; however, a friendly-looking short Frenchman with sandy blond hair jumped up to give me the *bise*. I returned his friendly greeting and reminded myself I'd come for the enjoyable company, not in pursuit of romance.

Shortly after our drinks were ordered, the musicians trickled out and set up in a space cleared of tables, not far from where we were seated. It was a good thing for the bar that we had come, as we were one of the few attendees who'd braved the cold. Parisians don't do well in below-zero temperatures, plus it was a Tuesday, and so not exactly the best night for drawing a crowd even in warmer months.

I chatted with the boys in between the sets of upbeat Senegalese tunes. Antoine recounted lively tales of his latest adventures in Krakow and Kiev before telling us about these new expat events he was organizing in Madrid. However, his parents were getting older and so he was considering moving back to Paris; as he said this last fact, he began trailing off and looking my way.

Hmmm... Was he looking for more incentive to move back to Paris, like I was currently doing for Canada? If so, he'd have to look for that reason elsewhere rather than across the table at me.

I changed the subject by sharing my latest news. While the new year had yet to bring me romance, it was actually bringing me other new things. Not only would I be starting to work full-time, managing the regional office for the cultural tour company I'd been doing some consulting work and tours for, I'd also accepted the presidency of the Canadian Ladies Association. The latter was a bit of a crazy commitment to make; I had too much on my plate already with the new job. Plus, working on my writing was about to be relegated to evenings and Sunday afternoons.

I seemed to be moving up in the world and my Paris life was coming together. I now had a job which roughly corresponded with my career goals and I was getting more involved in the local community. Could I give this up and move home after working so hard to and getting closer to achieving my dream life here?

Soon, the musicians grande finale of beating drums interrupted my wandering thoughts.

"We can take you home, Thomas has a car," offered Antoine on behalf of his friend, after he'd energetically applauded the bowing musicians, making a louder racket then their drummer. Thomas smiled broadly in agreement. I gladly accepted the offer. This way I wouldn't have to risk my life scurrying alone through those dimly-lit streets to the *métro*. Though, on second thought, I hoped Antoine didn't have any ulterior motives! I wasn't about to let them come up like the last time. With this freezing weather there was no question of having a 'relaxing' break in a park, either. However, nearing Montmartre, Antoine was struck by a moment of inspiration.

"Thomas, drive up to Sacré Coeur," he ordered. "It's such a beautiful evening, let's go admire the stars!"

It was a clear night; that was true. Even the clouds were staying in tonight, because it felt as cold as the Great White North!

Thomas obliged, and drove up the winding rue Lamarck to reach the mammoth white basilica where Antoine and I had last met. We parked the car and made our way to the lookout in front of the church.

"Isn't Paris *magnifique*..." declared Antoine, looking out at twinkling city.

"Yes, it's soooo... romantic..." murmured Thomas, looking in my direction. *Oh brother.* No, it wasn't romantic right then and there, even with the magnificent and magic view. *Don't get any ideas, Thomas,* I thought. He was a dirty blond version of Lionel: a sweet suburban engineer. *Come on romantic Paris! Where did your amorous spirit go? Can't you send me someone closer to what I was looking for?* My inner voice begged. I scanned the sparkling skyline, almost like I'd find the right gem if I looked hard enough out there; my eyes eventually landed on the West side of the view.

Maybe I could wait it out just a little bit longer for Viktor after all...

WINE... *NOT?*

LATE? TODAY? *Impossible.* We were going to one of my
favorite events of the whole year: the Independent Wine
Producers Fair. It was an oenophile's paradise, with over a
thousand independent winemakers from all over France
converging in one place. This was a bi-annual event; the
larger one was held at the end of November, while a smaller
event (still with around five-hundred exhibitors) was at the
end of March, so we were actually on this bacchanalian cloud
nine twice a year!

It was thanks to Special Kay that we'd originally
discovered the fair, all the way back in 2004. She'd received
two free invitations via her Master's program. At the time, it
seemed wine drinking was losing popularity amongst
France's youth; was giving free tickets to students an attempt

to combat this? Perhaps—they certainly had us hooked! After Kay'd given me the low-down on the event, I eagerly agreed. I could pop by in the afternoon with her before going to a birthday party I'd previously committed to. The fair sounded like great fun; little did we know just how fun it would be.

Always the meticulous one, Kay had done some advance research on the fair's website, picking out some of the most prestigious wine stands for us to visit. Arriving at the vast exhibition hall of the Porte de Versailles, we were struck by the beautiful sight of seemingly endless rows of winemakers serving up their delicious wares. We had all the good intentions of only stopping in at Kay's premium shortlist, but after six stands or so, and dozens of small samples of Grand Cru Bordeauxs, Burgundys and other unusual appellations we'd never heard of, our choice of stands became much more haphazard.

The hours were flowing by as freely as the wine. What was supposed to be a two-hour jaunt was turning into a four-hour meander. There was no way I was going to make it on time to a birthday party that was starting, well, right then. I naughtily called up the birthday girl and luckily got her voicemail; then I slurred out some pathetic excuse why I wouldn't be able to stop by. *Santé!* Kay and I carried on our sampling until the fair closed down at 8:00 pm. The evening ended with us swerving towards the *métro*, a few bottles in hand and what would become two throbbing heads the next morning.

The fair became a tradition of ours. Though unlike that first trip, each time we visited we became more and more savvy on how to tackle it, gradually bringing along bottled water; stickers to distinguish our tasting glasses; snacks to cushion the wine; and, most importantly, a trusted folding trolley to cart home a few cases of our favorite finds from the fair, just like the other pro attendees sported. With our improved strategies, our objectives also become more refined. We didn't attend so we could drink as much free wine as we could. On the contrary, we were advancing our wine education by discovering new grape varietals, the intricate details of the winemaking process and barrel loads of other fascinating facts about the beverage of the gods. We'd often joked it could be a good venue to meet someone, knowing that we'd at least share a common love of wine. However, the true highlight was not the tasting and tracking down of wonderful new wines; it was our lively discussions with the passionate winemakers that made our day. Some of these *vignerons* became our friends over the years and not a wine fair would go by without visiting them at their vineyards. Among this group of fair friends was Maurice.

We must have happened by his winery's stand a few years back, drawn in by its prestigious Châteauneuf-du-Pape sign, my all-time favorite red wine. This prestigious wine was grown on what had once been the vineyards of the popes during the period they'd been based in Avignon in the 14th Century. Those Popes had certainly appreciated its divine velvety bouquet. Today, its steep price tag put it out of reach as an 'everyday' wine. Therefore, the occasions when I did get to savor some—like those fancy dinners with the stylish

Italians—were all the more memorable. We girls must have already been a little tipsy by the time we weaved our trolley up to their counter at that particular fair, our jovial dispositions met by the equally jovial wine merchant. This was Maurice, an adorable, short, middle-aged fellow who we learned was the wine house's the sales manager. Along with him was the vineyard's owner, a tall, younger, blond man with a twangy South of France accent. Despite his presence, we spoke mostly to vibrant Maurice.

He went through his standard introduction of their various wines accompanied by a splash of each, beginning with a more simple Côtes-du-Rhône, and then working his way up their range, culminating in their sensational, satiny Châteauneuf. Soon, we were on a first name basis with him, and in addition to the regular tasting anecdotes, he entertained us with silly wine-inspired jokes and extra slashes of their prized beverage of the popes. With his generous laughter—and even more generous bottle pours—Maurice had seduced us into buying a couple of bottles and to adding his stand to our list of 'wine fair darlings.'

This particular year must have marked the second or third time Pussycat, Naughty and I had attended the fair along with the Countess. It was her distinguished tastes that led her to the brilliant idea that we could make the most of the fair by attending both Friday and Saturday afternoons. On Friday, we'd try to slip out of work early to be at the fair at 5:00 pm with the sole goal of sampling champagne. This would serve as a delicious—and free—*apéro*. Then we'd come back on Saturday for a more serious tasting of whites and reds.

So, as we were bubbly-ing our way through the stands at the 'smaller fair' that Friday, stopping in at only the gold-labeled champagne region stands, we happened upon Maurice's stand and took the opportunity to explain we'd be back the next day. He was absolutely thrilled to see us and blew us kisses as we giggled away, calling back over our shoulders: *à demain!*

As promised, we did return to his stand the following afternoon. Since we'd been getting to know Maurice better, our time spent at his stand became longer and longer each time; we were now easily spending twenty minutes testing out the latest batches and listening to his exciting stories, so we often made time for Maurice in the last stretch of the fair's opening hours.

Chuckling away at his latest tale, the dreaded announcement echoed through the building's P.A. system advising that the fair would shortly be closing its doors, so would all the drunken attendees stumble towards the exits.

"*Quel dommage!*" proclaimed Maurice, throwing his arms up in sorrow. "What a shame we have to end our great conversation!"

"It's always a fun time with you, Maurice," I cheered, savoring the last drops of the Châteauneuf left in my glass.

"Oh really?" he replied, sending a big smile straight my way. "Well, I should be finished early on Monday; perhaps we could carry on our discussion over dinner?"

"Come on, Lily! Take one for the team!" the Countess hissed into my ear. *Take one for the team?*

"Maybe, he'll have leftover wine to give you?" snuck in Pussycat. "Or you can get a free case of Châteauneuf the next time they are passing through?"

"I highly doubt it!" I seethed back. That wine was worth its weight in Bacchanalian gold.

The idea of having any free bottles was certainly more than a drop tempting; they might have a few opened tasting bottles to give away at the end of the fair. So with Pussycat's and The Countess' encouragement, and the wine hazing over my better judgment, I gave him my number and told him to give me a call.

It wouldn't hurt to grab a bite with Maurice, would it? We were just going out as friends after all, right? He couldn't have any other 'intentions' for getting together, other than having a little company on his last night in Paris and celebrating after an intense five days at the fair. *Bien sur que non.* Or so I'd convinced myself…

I told Maurice I could meet him nearby his hotel, which happened to be in the southern Montparnasse district. Like Montmartre to the north, it was once a sleepy suburb of a burgeoning metropolis until outdoor dance halls beginning springing up during the glory days of the French Revolution. In 1840, the neighborhood gained its first major building, le Gare de Montparnasse. This was the train station that served the south and west of the country. This new means of transportation brought an influx of Bretons to the capital and it was around this convenient gateway home where they naturally settled. With them came their regional specialty, *la crêpe*, and before long, the small streets around the station filled with tiny animated *crêperies*, decorated with lace doilies, cider jugs and pictures of fishing boats at sea.

As quaint as some of these locales were, they were always chaotic; waiters shouted orders across the room to the kitchen; steamy *galettes* thick with diverse combinations of savory ingredients or sweet *crêpes* coated in *caramel beurre salée* were whipped across tables, all to the hearty cheers of *santé* bellowed from the tables crowded with groups of friends. I chose the loudest of these to meet at—aiming for the *least* romantic ambiance possible.

As soon as we sat down at our assigned microscopic two-person table, snug as a bug against our neighbors, I could tell this was not at all what Maurice had in mind; however, I pretended not to hear his gripes about the mediocre wine list and the lack of anything that resembled *haute gastronomie* on the menu. As we munched on our *galettes*, I kept the conversation light, asking how the Fair had gone and how the vines had fared that winter.

The one factor I hadn't considered in this very non-date restaurant selection was the fact that eating at a *crêperie* was almost always a rushed experience. So, after we'd finished our dessert *crêpes*, I shouldn't have been surprised when Maurice suggested carrying on our evening elsewhere.

"Let's go to Le Coupole," he proposed. That was more his style. The turn of the 19th-century dance halls of what would become le Boulevard du Montparnasse had evolved over the century into a collection of classy cafés and *brasseries* made famous by the artists and intellectuals who frequented them. Especially in the Roaring Twenties when you might have encountered the likes of F. Scott Fitzgerald, Ernest Hemingway, Josephine Baker or Pablo Picasso. These were not the typical places I would normally choose to dine in or even stop by for a coffee—at eight Euros a cup. Their prestige had earned them the right to charge extortionate prices, plus their all too classic menus usually had nothing for vegetarians except possibly a starter of *oeuf-mayonnaise...* Oh, and dessert, the course I was least fond of. However, on that night, going to Le Coupole would certainly just be for a drink, and they would surely have a wonderful wine list to suit Maurice's high standards.

"*D'accord*," I conceded. I'd actually never been inside this posh establishment, so this would be the ideal occasion to go, and for free.

Maurice paid the meager bill at the *crêperie* and off we strolled the few blocks along the Boulevard until we reached the grand luminous facade of the legendary institution. Even though it was a Monday, the expansive dining room was still abuzz with black-tied waiters elegantly gliding to and fro, delivering plates of *foie gras, confit de canard* and bottles of grand cru wines to the café's refined clients. I was relieved to see there were no romantic little nooks here like across the street at Le Dome, where I could imagine Hemingway and Picasso had cozily wooed women. We were ushered to a comfortable table in the middle of the room, granting us a pleasant view of the theatrics of this glamorous café.

"Une bouteille de champagne," Maurice ordered without even looking at the menu. Was he merely celebrating the end of the wine fair... or were the bubbles meant for something else?

I really didn't know that much about Maurice, besides that he lived down in southern region of Provence and obviously loved wine. So over our bubbles, I heard extravagant stories of his past. We traveled back to his early twenties when he'd started off in the work world as a sailor and ended up marrying a flight attendant at a rather young age. One at sea, the other up in the skies... it was not a fantastic combination for a successful marriage, yet they did manage to have a couple of kids before getting divorced a few short years after their wedding.

Though he'd eventually gotten into wine, Maurice said it was more of a hobby to keep him busy. I'd just assumed he worked full-time as a sales rep for the wine company, however, he explained he mostly worked for them when they needed some extra manpower during the wine fairs. Instead, after permanently docking on land and giving up his marine career, he'd dabbled in inventions. He'd designed a building material made of recycled tires. He'd been the mastermind behind the little vacuum pump that keeps wine air tight and fresh, a logical invention given his work in the industry. Then, in a slightly similar vein, he'd come up with another little machine: *le aspiride*.

"*Le aspiride*?" I questioned, looking rather puzzled.

"Oui, le aspire-ride," he confirmed, dividing up the words. *Aspirer* was the French verb for vacuuming, and *une ride* was the word for… wrinkle? He'd invented a wrinkle vacuum?

"I use it myself, every day!" He exclaimed, describing how the infomercial-like gadget sucked up your wrinkles. "It really works! You can't even tell I'm sixty-nine."

Sixty-nine?!

Forget about the surprising invention, it was his age that was unbelievable. Maurice only looked around fifty, maximum fifty-five. His wrinkle vacuum really did work wonders. I needed a top up of my champagne to fully process all of this news I was suctioning in.

My astonishment only increased when he went on to tell me that through the children of his first marriage, he was already not just a granddad, but a GREAT granddad! I almost spit out my precious champagne! Yes, I'd heard him correctly. He was *un arrière grand-père*. Wow! I'd really had no intentions of dating Maurice from the get-go, and with this new information there was absolutely no way! So, he must have had kids really young… as did at least one of his children… and then his grandchild followed suit! Is this what happens with all the wine they drink in the South of France or did Châteauneuf-du-Pape have magical fertility powers? If the later was the case, I'd better steer clear of it!

His life story got crazier and crazier. In my state of bewilderment, he proceeded to tell me how he'd met his *current* wife (number *three*). A couple of years previously, his brother had been wooing a woman living in Brussels and he'd invited Maurice to tag along on his next trip up to see his *chérie*. It turned out, this wasn't a Belgian belle at all, but a cute, young Filipina who just happened to have a friend of hers visiting. Maurice fell instantly under the latter's charms, but that night was the eve of her return to the Philippines. He was so taken by her, he hopped on a plane a few days later to be with her.

"The young Filipina... How young is young?" I managed to ask in my increasingly dumbfounded state.

"Thirty-three."

So here was Maurice, a great grand-dad, married to a woman who couldn't have been much older than his granddaughter... and who was also virtually the same age as me. I didn't dare ask if he had kids with her, as his family tree was getting even more complicated than that of Count Hugues.

Our bottle of bubbly went down very fast especially with all of these incredible stories. When it was empty, Maurice gallantly insisted on driving me home despite my protests that it was a direct ride home on the *métro*. I'd much rather have gone home alone than be in a closed space with him, but he'd listen to no word of my protests. Plus, he said his vehicle was parked nearby.

At least there wasn't much traffic, so it was a comfortable and quick cruise up to Montmartre in his brand new Range Rover. I wasn't sure he really needed such a big vehicle, but I supposed he might need to drive through fields down in wine country or load the backseat up comfortably with his... *great* grandchildren! I doubted his salary from the wine company could cover the cost of the expensive SUV, so clearly his little inventions were doing well.

We crossed over the Seine and through Place de la Concorde, so beautifully lit at night. He happened to drop into the conversation he had a little apartment here in Paris, not far from the Champs Elysées, which was just to our left. Too bad that there was a renter in it or else he could let me stay there... *What? Why?* Did he use it as his *nid d'amour*—his little Parisian love nest? I didn't need a free place to live if it would surely involve some fringe benefits for Maurice, which he seemed to be insinuating. What about his cute young Filipina wife? Did he have mistresses in every port, true to his past life as a sailor?

"So no free bottles of Châteauneuf, huh?" sighed The Countess, looking depressingly into her average glass of Côtes-du-Rhône.

"He didn't even have a sample of his wrinkle vacuum kicking around in his car to give you?" asked Pussycat, adding insult to injury.

"Hey, what are you saying? I don't need his invention... quite yet," I defended. Actually, I would possibly as soon as I drifted further into my thirties. I made a mental note to Google where to buy one of his *aspirides* when the time came.

"The cad!" seethed Naughty, ever the stringent anti-cheating advocate. "His poor wife, stuck down in the Provence as he gallivants across the country selling wine and flirting with other women!"

"Maybe she's having an affair with a neighboring winemaker?" suggested The Countess, which garnered her dagger eyes from Naughty. "Or not…"

"At least you got a fully-stocked wine cellar of *grand cru* stories!" concluded Pussycat, trying to turn the conversation back to a positive note.

"Exactly. Besides, it wasn't like I had the slightest romantic interest in him," I reminded. "I was taking one for the team, *remember*? Why don't you go back to telling us all about this new guy you met, Naughty?" I threw in, attempting to change the subject.

Her eyes instantly lit up as she enthusiastically told us the story—for the fourth or fifth time now—of how she'd recently been charmed by a friend of her cousin's. This chance encounter now seemed to be blossoming into a great love story.

We were actually gathered over at the Countess' place to celebrate Naughty's return. She'd just come back from doing an internship in Toronto, four months too long for our liking. A freezing winter in Canada didn't seem like the most thrilling of prospects, although she'd kept warm—or rather her heart warm—with this new love interest. And it seemed serious. Serious enough to draw her back home? What would we do without our Naughty? I was trying not to panic, and calmed myself by remembering she still had a few months left to finish up her Masters. Perhaps the long distance wouldn't work, or she might land her dream job right here in Paris with this upcoming French degree in hand?

Who was I to fret over Naughty possibly leaving Paris? With this latest blow to my faith in Frenchmen (thanks, Maurice), I was longing more and more towards Viktor, who lived well beyond the borders of my current city. Would I really consider leaving France for him… or for *anyone*?

Mulling over this idea during the weeks following the wine fair, my heart skipped a beat when I opened my inbox to see a message from him.

From: Viktor   Sunday, April 24 2010 11:54:40 AM
Subject: Birthday Card Response - Shoulder check before opening

Hey Lily,

I couldn't wait, so thought I would send this along in response to the birthday card you so kindly sent.
This picture was taken as a timed shot especially for you in Malaysia some months ago. I am misbehaving, but it seems to come naturally. Look over your shoulder before you open:)

Xoxo Viktor

Oh my! Even with his warning I wasn't expecting the image that popped up when I clicked on the photo attachment. Amidst a gorgeous setting of a waterfall and lush forest… was the back of a tall, fit Viktor. Naked. Oh my, indeed! Getting over my initial shock, I was able to admire his sexy body. Wow! Maybe I could really move back home for that gorgeous figure? I mean... for that smart, interesting... nice guy?

As this dreamlike state was wearing off, a detail from his message jumped out at me. Why had he gone to Malaysia... and not come to Paris instead? Didn't he want to see me as badly as I wanted to see him? I was beginning to think my lofty dreams of something eventually happening with Viktor were drifting far out of reach, perhaps somewhere over the South China Sea?

LA CONVOCATION

Hi Lily,

My ex-husband might be stopping by,

if he does, could you give him this key?

Merci - Nicki

HMMM… COULD IT BE? Might I have a chance to meet Nicki's mysterious ex? Little did I know what her key was going to unlock!

I never really understood what exactly our glamorous American landlady Nicki currently did for a living. A former model turned fashion designer, the only thing I knew for certain was she no longer had her own fashion line since our office occupied what had once been her workshop.

At the beginning of the year, I'd been tasked with finding a newer, bigger office for the tour company I worked for. I truly hadn't been expecting to find anything exceptional, but it was love at first *click* when I stumbled across the Craigslist ad for a bright, spacious room, a stone's throw from rue Montorgueil, the trendy, centrally-located market street where I'd met Lionel for our first date. Though geographically and spatially perfect, it came with its share of intrigues... and surprises.

The whole space had once been a single apartment, Nicki had the front section and we had the quieter back section facing the courtyard. We each had our own entrance doors, so we only saw each other occasionally when crossing paths in the shared kitchen and bathroom. Despite the fact that signs with the respective company names hung on our doors, since ours was first, we often had deliver boys knocking at it bearing mysterious packages from Chanel, Louis Vuitton and Gucci for Madame Nicki. Letters were also slipped under our door addressed to one of her various businesses... or to a certain mysterious Mr. O'Brian. This was not her last name, or at least what she'd told us her last name was. At first, she referred to him as her 'business partner,' however, later on she let it slip that he was indeed her ex-husband. It was strange to me she was already divorced, as she barely looked thirty. Had she married a gay French fashionista so she could get residence papers? Unlikely. O'Brian didn't sound in the slightest French. Yet another slip of the tongue, revealed he was as Irish as his name suggested. Even better than my previous hunches, I imagined that she'd married him to get a European passport *and* at the same time cleverly evade France's astronomical business taxes. All my theories resurfaced while reading her note. Today I might just get a chance to meet 'Monsieur Ex Hubby'... and piece together the obscure puzzle of Nicki that preoccupied my overactive imagination.

I put the key on the corner of my desk and got down to work. That was about as much thought I gave to it until her doorbell startled me out of my digital depths in the mid-afternoon.

My eyes first shot in the direction of her door, then to the key. *Ah ha!* That must be *the* Mr. O'Brian! Had it not been for Nicki's note, I would have merely ignored her ringing doorbell. Mr O'Brian might not have realized which doorbell he should be ringing to acquire the key.

I hopped out of my chair, smoothed down my dress and went to my door. Flinging it open expecting to find a stylish, red-headed Irishman, a very tall, dark-haired rather ordinary looking man swung around instead.

"Bonjour Madame, Inspecteur Cluzot, Préfecture de Police."

A policeman? The plain-clothed officer confidently strode across the landing towards me, flashing an official looking badge.

"Is Madame Swanson here?"

"Ahhh ummm *non*..." I stammered. Wow, how many secrets did Nicki actually have?

"Can I leave you this *convocation* for her?" He politely requested.

I was 'allowed' to pick up and leave on the kitchen table all the letters erroneously delivered to our office. However, Nicki got terribly annoyed when I'd signed for certified letters or packages on her behalf unless she'd specifically told me in advance something would be coming. There was no mention of the police in her note! What could she possibly have to hide?

"*C'est rien*. It's nothing serious," he added, sensing my anxiety. "She was broken into a while ago and we just need her to stop by the station to clarify some details."

Broken into? At her home? Or *here?* We rarely locked the door between our offices and the last thing I wanted to add to my list of worries was the threat of burglary. He gave me a reassuring smile and I felt I had no choice but to oblige.

"Come in," I invited, still a little flustered. "Would you like some coffee? Water?"

"No, but thank you very much, it'll just take a few minutes for me to fill in this form," he replied, taking a seat at our meeting table. He reached into his jacket and produced a small, old fashioned pad, the kind with three different colored carbon sheets. Judging from its size, I figured that it shouldn't take too long to complete, so I hovered a few steps away instead of returning to my desk.

"Your name, please?" *Why did he need* my *name?* "It's merely a formality, since you're taking the convocation for Mrs. Swanson."

Maybe this hadn't been such a good idea after all. However, now it was too late, so I proceeded to reply to his question, spelling out my impossible foreign name, each letter printed with meticulous precision on the first dotted line. He was v.e.r.y. slow. They mustn't teach note taking in the French Police Academy. What happens if they are at an urgent crime scene? I guess this is why Nicki had to go back to give them more details; something had obviously been missed by the original, equally turtle-paced *policier*.

"Address?" *Geez*, that form was more comprehensive than I'd gathered from my quick glance. Then again, the French do love their paperwork and bureaucracy. This should have come as no surprise to someone who'd spent hours at the *préfecture* over the years, delivering the mountains of paperwork required to renew my annual residence permit.

"So, what do you do?" he enquired next, pen matched up to a blank line. Why should he need my profession? This opened up a whole new can of inquisitive worms and a series of off-the-record questions from the Inspector.

"*Hmmm*... today's date is...?" This question allowed me to escape back to my desk to double check this on my computer calendar. I proceeded to park myself there, I resigned to the fact, at this rate, it would take the Inspector a minimum of five to ten minutes more. Would he have to take down my age, eye color, height and weight as well?

"Are you English?" *Nationality couldn't possibly be a category on his form!* French people always think I'm British since I don't have the typical *Québécois* accent the French expect from a Canadian, nor do I have a typical 'American' accent. Therefore, my sing-songy voice is usually assumed to be from across the English Channel, not the Atlantic Ocean.

This was another off-topic question, which forced more polite conversation. I was starting to get a little antsy, noticing the growing number of unread emails piling up in my inbox.

"Right," he said getting back to his form. "I need your phone number... just in case we need to reach you..." Why would they need to reach *me*? Wasn't this convocation for Nicki? Again, I didn't really feel I could say no; therefore, another slow minute went by as I carefully enunciated the digits of my cell phone number, which he slowly repeated back. He then silently and painstakingly checked over his entire form.

"Oh I forgot, one last question, is it *madame* or... *mademoiselle*?" *Oh brother, the French!* No neutral 'Ms.' in this country. You're either married or you're not.

"Mademoiselle," I had to honestly answer.

Finally his form seemed to meet his rigorous standards of completion. He fastidiously tore off one of the sheets while unhurriedly rising from his seat, cueing me to his imminent departure. I walked over expecting a courteous farewell and the pink slip from his form pad, but he was lingering.

"Well if you need anything, just let me..." I started.

"*Vous êtes ravissante*," he passionately proclaimed cutting me off mid sentence. *Ravishing?* The French and their ardent amorous compliments! Wait a second... was he hitting on me? *Oh mon Dieu!* He now knew all my basic details, including that I was a *mademoiselle*, and thus proposition-able.

Sputtering out a *merci*, my cheeks most certainly beamed brighter than the red lights of a police car.

"Would you like to go to the movies tomorrow night? I have two free passes," he invited. *Talk about direct!*

"I'm really sorry, but I already have plans," I embarrassingly stuttered.

"You just don't want to go out with me."

"No, no, I really have plans," I defended, falling into his trap.

"How about next Tuesday?"

"Ahhh, ummm, maybe?" I really didn't know what else to say. Besides, since he now knew all my basic details, he could stake out both my home or office!

"Great! If I call you, you promise you'll answer?" *Is he going to add this to his form, too?*

"Of course," I solemnly pledged.

Whether I'd accept to go out with him or not was another story, but I had to give him credit for his audacity... and I thought that the potential prospects of a date would be the only way to make him leave. He smiled widely and bid me a *bon weekend*.

Well, that certainly added some spice to my Friday afternoon! About an hour later—in my rush to tie up any loose ends so I really could have *un bon weekend*—my phone rang, flashing an unknown number.

"*Allo?*"

"Mademoiselle Heise? C'est l'Inspecteur Cluzot." Holy smokes! Already? Geez, what could he possibly want now? "I forgot to ask you your birthday."

"Why do you need my birthday?" I asked. Was this just a false pretense to contact me?

"Oh, it's required for the form." He answered.

Once again, I felt hesitation in responding, not thinking to cross-reference my pink copy to see if it was actually on it.

"So about Tuesday, do you think you're free? I'd really like to see you again…" Persistence can pay off. He won his date.

"A cop?" exclaimed Naughty.

"Not a cop, an inspector," corrected The Countess, always attentive to status.

"Don't you remember what happened the last night you dated a man of the ranks?" reminded Pussycat, one eyebrow raised.

It was the Sunday after the Inspector had shown up at my door. After weeks of rain, the sun had managed to burst through the clouds so *les filles* and I were lapping up some rays and some rosé wine while lounging on the grass of Place des Vosges. We were not the only ones with the same idea. The pretty square framed by elegant red brick townhouses was a magnet for Parisians on sunny days and we'd barely managed to eke out a tiny patch of grass to lay down our little blanket. It wasn't very far from The Countess' apartment, so today it was serving as her not-so-private back yard.

"Yeah, you definitely do *not* want a repeat of lustful Lucien!" highlighted Naughty.

"Ah, well, the police is not the same as the *gendarme*," was my pathetic attempt to defend accepting of his date invitation. They had a point. There was no way I could forget Lucien, the fervent military policeman who'd taken a battle-like approach to wooing me a few years back. His weapon might have just been his cell phone, and its bullets his ardent amorous text messages, but he skillfully used them to bombard me daily for months. While he could have been applying some technical strategies learned during his days at military college, I'd put his blazing behavior mostly down to his passionate personality. Okay, there was a certain degree of Frenchness as well, the *coup de foudre*—the case of falling instantly madly in love. Was this what had happened to the Inspector?

"Don't worry, girls," I said, trying to put out their fears by pouring them some more rosé. "He might be a cop, but there's absolutely no way he's a great grandfather. That's better than the last date I went on, isn't it?" Yikes, from their expressions, obviously not. "He seems like a really nice, normal guy. Normal, I mean, not overly eager and suffocating like Mr. Militaire."

"Normal, huh?" questioned The Countess. "Would you be satisfied with 'normal'? Don't forget how awful you were to the sweet 'normal' engineer."

Ouch! She'd never forgive me for the disappearing act I'd played on the man she'd deemed to be Mr. Perfect.

"It's just one date, sergeant!" I exclaimed. "Plus, I promise to report back about how it goes... on the double!"

INSPECTOR CLUZOT [05/03/2010 11:42 AM]
Bonjour, it's Inspector Cluzot, from the police.Are we still on for tomorrow?
I hope so :)

I actually hadn't been out on a proper date in quite some time, well, other than my evening out with Maurice (and I didn't want to count that as a date, anyway). I had to admit, I was a little nervous, and also somewhat hopeful. Had fate finally sent the right person *and* straight to my doorstep? Express mail from the Gods! That would definitely be a letter I'd sign for, addressed to me or not. Of course, it would depend on what he was really like outside of our odd introduction, but I was approaching our encounter with an open mind.

The 'first date jitters' crept over me as I walked the ten minutes to our rendezvous point in front of a movie theater not far from the glitzy Opera Garnier. The area was once the city's glamorous entertainment district. Over a century later, most of the once fashionable 19th-Century cafés which bordered the wide boulevards, had been taken over by French and international restaurant chains. The plays and operettas, which had once been performed on the stage at its historic theaters, had largely been replaced by Hollywood blockbuster movies and big name Broadway musicals. I didn't normally hang out around there, but it was close to my office and to his police station. Well, that wasn't *quite* true; I did used to frequent one place in this neighborhood: the Pont d'Amsterdam. It was the lively Dutch bar where my wild university 'semester abroad' friends and I went for their international student night. It was also where I'd met Bad British Brad, the party boy U.N.E.S.C.O. worker who'd come up previously in conversation with the girls, when I'd met Italiano Mario.

When I passed our old Dutch hangout en route to meet the Inspector, I couldn't help but smile at the fact the bar was located right next to his Police Station. It was very possible that I'd also crossed paths with a younger version of Inspector Cluzot. Now those days seemed light years away. Our Saturday evenings had quieted quite a bit not only since then, but also in the recent year with the most eager dancer of the bunch, Naughty, being away on her internship. The playbill of my nights out now headlined with rosé chez The Countess, elegant dinners, champagne at sophisticated cocktail parties, or drinks in fancy cafés. Was there still a yearning in me for dancing on tables and being a little naughty, or was La Tigresse being tamed?

"Bonsoir Mademoiselle."

I was yanked out of my nostalgia by the friendly greeting of the Inspector, as he awkwardly leaned down from his tall height to bestow me with a kiss on each cheek. We barely knew each other (well, he knew a lot of personal details about *me*), but the standard French cheek kiss greeting still seemed appropriate.

"I don't think I told you my first name! It's Benoit," he added. Okay, now I knew one more thing about him. And over the course of the evening I would learn much, much more...

We made some casual small talk as he acquired our tickets for the latest French hit, what was supposed to be a comedy about an aging Frenchman trying to seduce a much younger woman... sigh! This was a recurring theme in France and one I was trying to avoid more than ever! At least Inspector Cluzot, or rather, Benoit, didn't appear much older than me, unless he had one of Maurice's *aspiride* machines! That was extremely unlikely, unless the police at his *Commissariat* had come across some contraband *aspirides* in a raid. Although, I doubted there was a huge trade in these smart devices on the Parisian black market.

The movie wasn't all that bad, but it reinforced my firm stance on steering clear of grandpa-mistress seeking types. The nice weather we'd lapped up on the weekend had lingered, so after the movie Benoit suggested we amble back towards our workplaces. There we'd surely be able to find a nice table *en terrasse* for dinner and flee the chains restaurants near the movie theater. I highly approved of this proposal and took it as a sign he at least had decent taste. We found just the right outdoor table at a historic bistro, which had been converted into a hip Italian restaurant in this much cooler neighborhood than where we'd just come from. I was more than happy with Italian cuisine… that would leave the subject of my vegetarianism off the table for this first date.

Things started off very well. Benoit was vivacious and funny. Conversation flowed as smoothly as the soft evening breeze. However, in keeping with the season, there was the occasional gust of chilly air, accompanied by topics, which equally cooled my prospective interest in my date.

The first of these topics was his family. I shouldn't have been surprised when he told me he had kids. He must have been in his late thirties; the typical French wedding bells and family clock usually started ringing and ticking as people crept towards thirty. He had a boy and a girl, six and four respectively, so not too young, but not parent-evading teenagers either.

What about *Mrs.* Cluzot? Benoit went on to tell me he'd married an American (it seemed he had a weakness for foreigners!). At least they were divorced, unlike Count Hugues, with his married but ever-wandering eye. I had no concerns Benoit was lying, because he went on to tell me he'd been deserted by his ex.

Apparently, she couldn't handle suburban life, so she'd left him and the kids, hightailing it back to the city center. Back to Paris… I mention this because the second topic which made me a little *froide* was where he lived, Chantilly.

Yikes!

This was one of the last suburbs in the greater Paris metropolitan area, home of a fairy tale castle, but, like his ex, living so far away also didn't feature in my sort of fairy tale.

This was of course his side to the story and there might have been plenty of good reasons why she'd left. For example, maybe he had a very hairy back and refused to do anything about it? Wrote poetry by flashlight in a tent (Chantilly was surrounded by forests after all)? Had a collection of secret wives hidden away in other castle suburban towns? No wait… these flaws were already worn proudly by other sharks in the Paris dating waters.

He was probably a great father and had a lot to bear, what with raising his children virtually all by himself. Regardless, all of this did not bode well for our dating prospects. Still, I had resolved to keep an open mind. I tried to push these concerns aside for the immediate moment and instead enjoy the rest of our evening. We talked about other things, laughed, finished off our bottle of wine, and then he offered to drive me home (funny how the police didn't seem to mind having a few drinks and then driving). He was a complete gentleman, dropping me off without putting on any sly moves or attempting a more passionate kiss other than a farewell *bise*. He did slip in he hoped we'd be able to get together next Tuesday… if his sitter was available.

THE COUNTESS [05/11/2010 11:50 PM]
Soooo… How did it go? Did his use his neighborhood influence to get you into the Grand Vefour? Or at least Frenchie? Those places take months to get a reservation at, but a flash of his badge…

PUSSYCAT [05/011/2010 11:51 PM]
Is he as tactical as Mr Militaire? ;-)

NAUGHTY [05/11/2010 11:52 PM]
You'd better be at home
ALONE right now!

I really didn't know what to tell the girls. I sent a quick reply to dowse any wildfires. I left the facts I'd learned about his life for the next time I'd see them in person, preferably after a glass (or five) of wine to help me decide what to do about this romantic dilemma.

Over the next few days, Benoit sent me a couple of messages, which were *nothing* like the barrage I'd gotten from Mr. Militaire—this cop kept a straight line. He confirmed he could secure his babysitter for the following Tuesday and I agreed to a second date, however, having had some time to mull things over, doubts were mounting.

Did I really want to spend time in the suburbs, other than the occasional Sunday excursion to meander through castle gardens? Was he interesting enough? Could I be a stepmom at this stage of my life (or even in six months or a year's time)? I was hoping that seeing him again might answer some of these questions.

Once again, he chose a place in our mutual work district, this time suggesting we go for Japanese food on rue Sainte Anne, Paris' tiny Japantown packed with busy sushi and ramen noodle joints. I took this as another good sign, as it showed he had an interest in different cultures.

Well, on second thought, Parisians tend to be big fans of diet-conscious Japanese food, so it might have just been that… but I preferred to think of it as a testament to some worldliness on his part. It wasn't necessarily my first choice for dining out since I didn't eat fish, but there was usually something I could eat on the menu like vegetarian maki or vegetable skewers. This meant I'd have to broach the subject of my vegetarianism, though it could be a good test to see how he reacted. When I admitted my dietary habits to the French, they usually first thought I was crazy, then immediately asked if I ate fish.

Walking by the more boisterous restaurants along the street—many of which had long lines snaking out their doors—Benoit seemed to know the perfect one to select. It was a quieter place which he seemed to know well, probably from lunching here with his colleagues, but who knows… might it be a favorite spot of his for dinners with other neighborhood girls he delivered 'convocation' to?

Unlike our first date, conversation was a little stalled and my worries that we didn't have much in common quickly resurfaced. Had I spoiled things with all of my overanalyzing? He seemed like a really nice guy; so couldn't I just stick it out… and try?

THE DANGERS OF TOO MUCH

SILLY SAUCE

From: TAD   Wednesday, May 19 2010 9:47 AM
Subject: re: Pretty Canadian seeking gala date

Heyyyyyyyyyyyyy!

I've been meaning to contact you! Thanks for getting in touch. No need to apologize for silly "behaviour" (you really ARE Canadian :). We all consumed the silly sauce, and it showed. Have to check the camera one of these days!

NORMALCY. Settling down. Life in the suburbs. *Stepmom-hood.*

These daunting thoughts were roaming through the maze of my confused mind, that is, until a couple of days later when a surprising exit magically appeared for me. And I fled that mental labyrinth… running in the polar opposite direction.

I really did hem and haw over whether or not I'd give Benoit one more shot. He was sweet, stable and secure exactly the kind of person the girls were trying to push me towards. Nevertheless, my inner wild child was protesting, restless and worried. 'Exciting' or 'international' were not exactly adjectives I'd use to describe him. Sure, he was certainly around a multitude of international people on a daily basis... panhandling Roma gypsies, illegal immigrants caught during spot checks around Les Halles, or Chinese prostitutes hauled in from rue Saint Denis (Paris' waning red light district). Still, this was not exactly the sort of international engagement or worldly allure I was craving.

This time it wasn't Viktor popping up to provide me with a convenient escape (though he was still very much pursuing me through that romantic maze in my head). The tables were turned on Benoit by the following invitation:

> GEMMA [05/13/2010 10:42 AM]
> Hey Lils....are you free tonight?
> There's this international writers'
> apéro, care to join me?

International writers? Now we were talking! There were definitely very good chances that some cute, smart cosmopolitan men would be amongst the attendees. To sweeten the invitation, the event was on the eve of one of France's famous long weekends of the month of May (some years there are, amazingly, up to four!), and it was taking place at a bar just down the street from my office. This was potentially why Gemma—a food writer friend—had invited me to tag along. It wasn't far from my office at all... but it was even *closer* to Benoit's police station! We'd only been out twice, and that could hardly be categorized as 'exclusive' yet. Therefore, I could go out for a guilt-free drink with a group of people, albeit which could potentially include cute flirt-worthy boys, right?

Luckily, I didn't have to pass in front of the *Commissariat* on my way to the address on rue du Sentier Gemma had provided. I'd certainly walked down this way numerous times, but I had never noticed there was a bar sandwiched between two of the street's dingy wholesale clothing shops. The obscure, industrial-like exterior hid a hip New York-style lounge featuring wide sofas, exposed ventilation ducts and cocktails served in vintage champagne *coupes*—one of which, was in my hand minutes after joining the cool bunch of scribes who penned for the English world's top publications.

Yes indeed, this really was more like it. I almost breathed a sigh of relief. It was a reminder I didn't need to settle for Benoit. If I wasn't into him; other, more fruitful opportunities could arise. This crowd certainly better fit the profile of what I was looking for.

About fifteen people from the four corners of the globe gradually trickled in, roughly an equal man-woman ratio. Fed by foreign correspondents for the *Wall Street Journal*, *The New York Times*, the BBC and CNN, our lively conversation bounced from world politics to the French President's latest girlfriend. The liquid in our glasses transitioned from cocktails to white wine, and the bottles seemed to increase with the decrease in attendees. It was supposed to just be an *apéro*, however, the clock's hands had somehow reached past 11:00 pm; Gemma and I were left in the company of half the original number of guests. Another bottle reduced the sum down to five.

"Who's coming back to my place? I've got champagne in the fridge." offered up the American journalist who'd organized the *soirée*.

"Oh man, I should have gone home hours ago," said Gemma. "I have an article due tomorrow. But you go ahead, Lily. Have fun!"

Well, I wouldn't be working in the morning due to the holiday, so tonight was like a Friday night. I could stay out late. I always had this fear of missing out on fun (and champagne), though the fact the American journalist who'd extended the invitation was cute gave me extra incentive to tag along.

I was handed a helmet and jumped on the back of his scooter, and we zoomed through the silent and dimly lit after-hours streets of Paris to reach his apartment in the Bastille area. We were joined shortly after, by the other couple of leftover *apéro*-goers. The four of us quickly downed the first bottle of chilled bubbly... the second was finished off by just two of us.

Oh man. My head felt like it had gone through the wringers... of a newspaper printing press.

Okay, maybe that last bottle hadn't been such a good idea. I peered out of the cracks of my eyelids. I was definitely not in Montmartre, nor was I in Kansas … even though my magic red shoes appeared to have taken me down the Yellow Brick Road of a new dating adventure. However, I wasn't entirely sure if this romantic Land of Oz necessarily contained rosier pastures (or rather poppy fields) than the one starring the suburban cop I'd just tapped my heels to escape from.

The proprietor of the bed I was in did seem to have a perfect profile—on paper. A writer for one of the most renowned American newspapers, he was around forty, extremely fun and, to top it all off, was very witty and worldly. All the makings of a happy ending, right? I was just embarking on this new road, so I couldn't let my mind get too carried away in these lofty dreams of reaching the Emerald 'Amorous' City controlled by this new Wizard. As with Dorothy, I may need to overcome some challenges along the way, at least I had my own set of trusted companions to help me: my lady friends.

Staying overnight—or rather the few hours that had remained of the night—after just meeting someone it is usually considered bad form. That is, if one is hoping for more than one night of champagne and fun times. The rules, however, were quite different in Paris where passions are pursued more easily (and can live on past dawn) than in more rigid Anglo-Saxon countries. Actually, while I thought there could be decent prospects with the journalist, the whole evening had been a complete surprise, so I sort of didn't even know what to expect.

I didn't stick around too long after waking up with my pounding head resting on his broad chest, mostly due to my crying eyes, stinging from sleeping with my contact lenses in. I bid him *à bientôt* and squinted along the Yellow Brick Subway Lane up to the Land of Montmartre, where I eventually soothed my eyes—and aching head—in my own bed on this French holiday.

I thought I'd given him my number the previous night (or possibly just my business card), but my memory was having trouble seeing through the haze of the night's follies. Therefore, after a week of no news, I decided to take matters into my own hands. I cleverly remembered while I didn't have his number, I did have his email from the message Gemma had forwarded to me with the details of the *apéro*.

I also had the perfect premise to contact him: an invitation to join me at an elegant charity event organized by the Canadian Ladies' Association at the Canadian Ambassador's house. Champagne and glitzy chandeliers seemed to be an appropriate date setting for him. Nothing ventured, nothing gained! Plus, as President of the Association, I thought I'd look pretty posh showing up with a successful journalist! This was more how I'd envisioned the direction of my Paris life: running towards exciting cultural events in the city, and away from the hum-drum suburbs.

From: TAD   Wednesday, May 19 2010 9:47 AM
Subject: re: pretty canadian seeking gala date

Heyyyyyyyyyyyyy!

I've been meaning to contact you! Thanks for getting in touch. No need to apologize for silly "behaviour" (you really ARE Canadian :). We all consumed the silly sauce, and it showed. Have to check the camera one of these days!

Your offer is lovely--and the venue/occasion sound quite regal-but I have a friend in town from Thursday to Sunday next week and have to play guide, host and sherpa. :(Another time??????????

In other news, how the devil are things????

Rock on, Tad

Rock on? Well, it seemed I wouldn't be 'rocking on' with him in the immediate future. However, he did seem to have a fair excuse. His message was friendly and he genuinely seemed like he want to see me again. What to do, then?

From: TAD   Wednesday, May 19 2010 8:40 PM

Amsterdam will rule. Lucky you! I will be writingwritingwriting about Copenhagen and Bordeaux. You will be chilling along canals and taking hookers to smoke weed in Anne Frank's house. Awesome.

Have fun!!!!!! I will keep you in mind next time I'm near Reaumur!

X, Tad

"He will 'keep you in mind the next time he's near Reaumur'?? What kind of follow up is that?" tisked The Countess.

"Um well, not a particularly great one." I replied woefully.

"That's putting it mildly!" tacked on Naughty. Here we were sitting on one of the sunny terraces near my office, this time at our favorite café on rue Montorgueil. If I couldn't be having *apéro* around my office with Tad, the girls were always reliable and very willing participants.

"We're near Reaumur right now; maybe it's us who should give him a call?" dared Pussycat, reaching for my phone next to my glass of rosé.

"Don't even think about it!" I hissed, scooping it up and jamming it to the bottom of my purse. "Besides, I don't even have his phone number. Maybe he won't ever contact me again, but I couldn't bear the thought of being tied down with a serious, straight-laced suburbanite." I attempted in my defense. The Countess and Naughty sighed in exasperation. They were not highly fond of my decision to forget about Benoit. "Don't you guys think Tad's a better match for me? He's a regular contributor for one of the world's most prestigious newspapers. He's traveled the world! He doesn't live in the 'burbs… and he doesn't have kids!"

"Well, not that you—or potentially even he, know of…" Pussycat slid in, mischievously.

"And all of that won't really matter if he doesn't contact you again," reminded The Countess.

I was hopeless at these sorts of situations. I supposed my mistake, after staying over, was in giving Tad an open invitation to redo *apéro* together, if he was ever nearby my office. I should have come up with another premise to meet up, but I didn't want to seem desperate either. If he wanted to see me, he could take some initiative. That was, if his and my upcoming travels didn't impede things.

"Let's put the forty-something American aside. I'm more interested in knowing if you'll be hanging out with your dreamy Dutch friend, while you're in Amsterdam!" Pussycat piped, thankfully changing the subject.

No, I wasn't going off to Amsterdam, on the next May long weekend, to rendezvous with the to-die-for Dutch boy I 'hung out' with whenever I was up in his fabulous city. Rudolf wasn't to be confused with bad Dutch-Canadian Mario. He was a friend of my university roomie Wilhemina and we'd known each other for easily eight years or so. The thought of his beauty often sparked me to contemplate moving to Amsterdam, thoughts usually drowned out by memories of Holland's dismal weather. However, Rudolf's wonderfulness was enough to brighten up any grey day. So, I was hoping we'd at least be able to meet up for a drink, though considering why I was going up there, I wasn't sure I'd have any free time whatsoever.

The schedule for my childhood British friend Mina's bachelorette party—or 'hen do' as the Brits call them—look quite packed with embarrassing activities, including dressing the bride-to-be up in tacky costumes, trying to keep the dozen of drunken partygoers from falling into the canals, stumbling into and out of coffee shops, and God only knows what else (well, He most certainly wouldn't condone what we were going to do!).

After that, I'd only be back for a few weeks before heading up to England for Mina's wedding (each year my holiday plans tended to revolve around at least one nuptials). This could possibly keep me from seeing Tad for an even longer period of time. We hadn't yet gotten around to talking about his summer plans, which could very well be taking him to many work or holiday destinations... and into the pathway of countless beautiful and exotic girls.

> From: Viktor   Saturday, May 29 2010 7:15 PM
> Subject: re: Would you be my date?
>
> Hey there Lily,
>
> Thanks so much for your offer to tag along to the wedding with you. I won't be able to slip off to Europe this summer, but maybe in the fall? Are you coming back this way at all for the summer? Would be great to see you... and get a special birthday card in advance?
>
> Xoxo Viktor

In all honesty, the person I'd much rather be spending my summer with was Viktor. I wasn't surprised he didn't take me up on my invitation. After all, he didn't know the bride and groom, I was just fishing around for a pretext to reach out to him. Would he really consider coming over in the autumn? One of these days I might have to take some more daring steps to make him open up. However, I couldn't help but hope he would act first...

MERDE

THE REST OF my summer was rather flat on my romantic horizon. It was like I was lost, wandering a barren desert. There was nothing but radio silence from Tad. Then I had a momentary respite at a Dutch oasis in the form of a beer with Rudolf, whose cuteness never ceases to make me woozy! This is dangerous in situations of draught! Mid-month I was treated to a mirage of Viktor in the form of a photo-less birthday message (his camera was broken). I did get my hopes up that even this small token from Viktor appeared to maintain my faith and guide me out of this wasteland—with him as my prize for surviving this arduous journey. However, it only led me to England where I got disgustingly hit on by my friend's fiancé on the eve of their wedding!

These events all left me with a bitter feeling my whole summer had been wasted, including the desire to never, ever want to get married.

That is, until early September, when I received a pleasant and unexpected email from Tad:

From: Tad   Friday, September 3 2010 5:36 PM
Subject: Heyyy!

Greetings from Beirut!
I've been living here for two months. Might stay forever. :)
How is all in Paris???? Triumphs? Tragedies?
Hope all is smooth with you.

Send news when you can...
Tad

At first, my heart skipped a beat when I saw his message. I must have been on his mind, right? Then I reread his message. What was this about 'living in Beirut'? Did that mean he didn't actually 'live' in Paris? He might stay... *forever?* Geez, I wasn't really sure what to make of him. However, it seemed like he was taking a bit of an 'out of sight, out of mind' approach. We exchanged some friendly emails, but I was beginning to wonder if my eyes would ever lay sight on him again? Maybe. As it would turn out, I did get another message from him a few weeks later:

From: Tad   Monday, October 1 2010 3:57:52 PM
Subject: Here and Gone Again...

Friends, Amis, Asdeeqa,

I am back from three months in Lebanon and am eager to see all of you, so I'm having people over on Friday night. I hope you can   all make it, as I'll be leaving for NYC less than a week later.

The evening promises a formidable quotient of power, awesomeness, chips, champagne and high-fives. Also music. And lots of old friends. Mark your calendar.
See you soon!!!
Tad

Sure, it was a message from him, but one sent en masse to half or even all of the English-speaking writing community in Paris; at least I could take solace in being added to this list. A small grain of hope something could happen with him was struggling to remain planted in my heart. Although, it might have been drowned with too much champagne, or as Tad had called it, silly sauce.

It was far from the ideal situation, as I'd already been invited to two other parties that night. Nevertheless, I didn't want to miss this opportunity, especially since it seemed like he was going to New York City right afterwards. *Mon Dieu*, would that be another three-month trip? I R.S.V.Ped and was granted a peppy reply from Tad, filled with his now trademark overabundance of exclamation marks. Would he be that enthusiastic to see me in person?

The other slight complication was that one of the other parties I was going to that night was the birthday celebration of a very close friend of Gemma's, Annie. She was another food writer whom I also knew. It hadn't hit me right away, but my memory drudged up something Gemma had dropped into a previous conversation around six months prior to the May *apéro* when I'd met Tad. We were in a fancy wine shop and she was trying to pick out a present worthy of the fortieth birthday of a writer that Annie had her sights on. Could that have been... Tad? There were actually fairly good odds it was. I looked at the guest list and, sure enough, both Gemma and Annie were on it. That conversation in the wine shop had occurred quite a while before I'd met him, and besides, Gemma hadn't referred to him by name. Plus, it wasn't like Annie had said anything to me directly about her and Tad, so I hadn't done anything wrong. It would merely be a tiny bit awkward if Gemma had mentioned to Annie I'd scooted off with Tad that night.

Since Annie was having her own party that night, it was certain neither she nor Gemma would be at Tad's. Their absence would ensure no potentially uncomfortable moments between us at his party. It also meant I might need a wing-woman to go with me. That would be a complicated invitation since I'd be dragging the willing party-goer to two or three parties over the course of the night. A quick second scan over the guest list and my eye caught the name of one other person I knew, Clarisse, a photographer friend. *Whew!* I wouldn't be wandering the room trying to encroach upon the conversations of strangers. I would start at Annie's party and discreetly slip away to Tad's before midnight, just like Cinderella, albeit without the magical *citrouille* carriage.

Arriving on the earlier side at Annie's party, I was warmly greeted by the birthday girl and happily chatted away with the various people I knew in attendance. When I did get ready to drift off around 11:00 pm, Annie bid me farewell with a broad smile and a chipper "Have fun at Tad's party!"

Crap.

It seemed like she was in the know after all... and my hunch about her and Tad was most likely true. I stuttered something along the lines of "I have a different party to go to as well" (which I really *did*... but was planning to skip out on), and tried to escape without a massive cloud of shame hanging over me.

I arrived shortly before midnight to find the party in full swing; Tad's two-room apartment was overflowing with a lively group of international media types. He gave me a friendly hello, put a glass of 'silly sauce' into my hand and was just as soon off to greet the latest newcomer. I found Clarisse among the partygoers and I enjoyed hearing about her latest photo projects in Africa. Maybe all these media types were constantly bopping all over the world?

Clarisse eventually went to track down a refill of champagne. In the interim, I carried on gabbing with a young filmmaker, who'd joined us by the window where he'd gravitated to have a smoke. He told us he'd met Tad that previous summer in Beirut, where they'd been in the same Arabic class. I couldn't quite tell where he was from, though from his features, I guessed he was either Mexican or from Central or South America. This hunch was reinforced when I finally learned his name: Alejandro. He was a bit on the short side, but he was still pretty cute and youthful; he couldn't have been over twenty-six.

I didn't mind chatting with him, either. Tad was busy with his hosting duties and I didn't want to follow Clarisse around like a lost puppy. Plus, it felt good to have a 'new friend' to distract me from wondering what would happen with Tad. Alejandro told me all about his adventurous time in Beirut and his filming projects. I explained what I did for a living and I might have even told him my recent harrowing experience with my friend's fiancé at the wedding in England. Whatever we discussed, the conversation was fun and full of laughs. Forty-five minutes—possibly even an hour quickly passed by. Occasional other people floated by, briefly adding to our bubbly effervescent conversation or topping up our glasses with more bubbles.

"I need to go find some cigarettes; could you come with me?" he said. "I don't speak French and don't really know where we are…"

"Sure," I replied without giving his request much thought. We'd only be gone a few minutes, so no one (*Tad*) would even notice we were gone. I didn't even bring my purse seeing as we'd be back in a jiffy.

Soon enough we were giggling our way down to the bar on the corner of Tad's street; surely they'd have some cigarette packs tucked away in a drawer behind the bar, the secret after-hours tobacconists.

"Do you want to get a drink?" he offered, after I'd translated his cigarette order for him.

"Okay, why not?" I gave in easily. Not like we didn't have tons of free alcohol back at the party, and not like I really needed more to drink; however, this guy was fun to hang out with.

"Cheers!" We clanked our newly-shaken Mojitos, took a big chug, and plunked them down on the counter. That wasn't all that was about to come into my mouth… before I could realize what was happening, Alejandro's tongue was flirting with the pieces of mojito mint lingering on my own tongue! A very pro Che Guevara guerrilla love*fare* move! Maybe he was Argentinian? Or Cuban?

Holy guacamole! Hot tamales! What had I gotten myself into this time? I'd innocently gone out to help this poor—but admittedly sexy—foreigner buy some cigarettes! I'd been totally oblivious to any flirting coming my way. My fuzzy, boozy brain was now drowning in this unforeseen dilemma, when I had a chance to emerge from his sea of kisses! He might have been young-looking, but he was a darn fine, experienced kisser!

The crap from earlier in the evening was turning into some serious *mierda*. I'd come to the party to hook back up with the journalist, who—as it would seem—was a much more practical catch: he had an apartment in Paris and despite his travels, he did call the City of Light his home. He seemed to have his life pretty much together, unlike *signor* fluttering around the world making short movies. Plus, Tad was a better age match for me, not that I knew just how young this filmmaker was. I estimated that he was at least four, if not six or seven years younger than me. The biggest strike against the sexier Alejandro was that he was just breezing through town. Even if it turned out to be true love and we spent the whole weekend in each others' hypothetically adoring arms, it would most certainly only be for that one weekend. I was looking for more than just some passing *pasión*.

"Pleasseeee… let's go back to my hotel!" he begged, pulling at my sleeve in the direction of the bar exit.

Tad was far from a sealed deal. There had most likely been a bounty of beautiful babes in Beirut, right at his fingertips. Not to mention the many pretty girls at the party; how many were his ex-bedmates? Or, how many other hopefuls were waiting to pounce on him (or vice versa)?

My mind was swimming in circles.

"Come on..." Alejandro continued, adding another fervent kiss in a final effort of persuasion. It was true: he was cuter and much more eager to spend 'time' with me than the journalist had been that night, and actually, since we'd hooked up back in May.

"Alright..." I gave in slightly hesitantly.

Uh oh: Triple *mierda*! My purse. It was still back up at Tad's. I couldn't leave the area without it, because inside were my phone and house keys. I could just tiptoe back inside and grab it, couldn't I?

"I'll wait for you here," he said, as I entered the codes I'd previously written on my hand and climbed up the stairs, slowly creeping back into the apartment.

Quadruple *alqaraf*! I even had to throw in some Arabic crap, in light of where the two of them had met. Where the heck was everyone? I glanced around the room in mild horror to find about only four people remaining. How long had we been gone for? Now there would be no sneaking involved in this botched purse snatching.

"Ah, there you *arrreee*..." cooed Tad, suddenly oh-so-very friendly.

This was beyond crap, *mierda, merde* and *alqaraf*. What was I supposed to do? Now the other people were leaving and I was like a snake caught in the hypnotic power of its charmer. Was I going to have my intended catch after all? Tad really was the more rational choice. It was either rationality which had returned, or cowardice that took hold, but I stayed at Tad's, leaving the poor boy down at the entrance to the building. I had no idea how long he must have waited; ten, fifteen, twenty minutes? I did feel very terrible about it, but I was firmly constricted in this *merde*.

The next morning Tad had to get up early.

"I'm going out shooting with Ale," he said. I gave him a quizzical look and he continued. "You know, Alejandro, the filmmaker. I'd convinced him to pass by Paris on his way back to Colombia, so we could do some shooting around town together this weekend."

Could there really be a *fifth* crap? Oh my god, the probability I would come up in conversation was extremely high; guys talk about these sorts of things, don't they? Would Tad brag about his conquest, or keep it to himself? Would Alejandro be so annoyed with me that he wouldn't bring up his own defeat?

Luckily, Tad was going to pick up Alejandro at his hotel, so there was little chance of me running into him… downstairs. I was granted some lame, all-too-perky "See you when I get back from New York (!!!!!!!)" farewell, and off he went in one direction and I, meekly, in the other.

What a *merdique* mess I'd created! And besides, I was genuinely mortified for leaving Alejandro in the lurch. I should have just explained the complicated situation to him from the start. He'd just caught me *so* off guard. How could I apologize?

I wasn't about to text Tad to ask to speak to Ale (I *still* didn't have his number anyway!). However, Tad had this bad habit of not blind-copying everyone on his party invitation emails, so I figured it should be rather easy to find Ale's email. Sure enough, with a little detective work and double-checking on the internet I'd found the right guy, I sent him an attempted apology for my bad behavior. It wasn't a huge surprise that I never received a reply; I hope I had at least gotten to the right person, or else the receiver must have been downright perplexed!

If the boys had talked, would my chances with Tad really be kaput? I wasn't sure what Tad would have thought about it... he had won out in the end, so from his perspective, he shouldn't care... right? Or would he have thought I was nothing but a flighty flirt, which wasn't completely true? I hadn't done anything intentional to lead Ale on; I merely lacked the guts to react to his quick advances... and was just so indecisive I couldn't manage to pick one Yellow Brick

Road and follow its path. Apparently, it didn't really matter, as he was going off to New York and for who knows how long.

> From: Tad   Monday, November 8 2010 2:38 PM
> Subject: LAST-MINUTE PARTY!!!
>
> Dear Friends:
>
> Soon I will be a year older, and a year *awesomer*. As will Johnny.
>
> In recognition of such, we are hosting a party this Friday. Don't bring us any gifts--the presence of our FRIENDS is more than sufficient--but bottles of wine or champagne for the party are encouraged. :)
>
> RSVP. Hope to see you there!
> Tad!!!!!

Apparently his trip back to the States hadn't been as long as his summer stay in Beirut.

"Will you come with me? *Pleeeeease?*" I implored the Countess. This time I would not be going alone! I'd need a good wing-woman.

"I really don't think this guy is worth your while at all," she said disapprovingly. "He might be acclaimed on paper, but his 'get-in-touch' record is far less exemplary."

"Sure, I didn't get a personal message from him on his return, but he did include me on the invitation to the party which means he obviously wants me there, right?" I attempted to rationalize.

"Yes, you… and probably fifty other girls!" she blasted.

"Well, there's only one way to find out! Plus, there's bound to be a lot of champagne," I added, trying to make the invitation more tempting.

"Fine, I'll go, but mostly because I want to see what this guy looks like." The Countess was rather picky about the events she attended; it seemed like she now had two good reasons to tag along.

Even though I was beginning to think The Countess was right, that things were going nowhere with him, I felt I had to give it one more shot.

Dressed to my cutest, and bearing the gift of fancy champagne I'd scored on sale at my wine shop, I made my way over to the party, which was being held at an art gallery close to Tad's place. The Countess and I'd planned to be fashionably late, arriving around 9:00 pm. It might have been my imagination or my nerves, but I sensed that Tad was being a little standoffish from the start. He gave us a reluctant yet warm enough welcome, before quickly excusing himself to greet new arrivals. I couldn't quite put my finger on his behavior, but it seemed off. If he'd actually found out from Alejandro about our little 'excursion' to the bar and was annoyed about it, why had he invited me to the party? Did he just have a massive party invite list he added people to, but then forgot to take some undesirables off?

I noticed there was a large gaggle of girls in attendance. I was beginning to wonder how many of them he'd slept with and then kept dangling around. Like with me, perhaps he managed to retain them with the occasion overly-friendly email and the odd party invitation; events where they'd be hopeful for some of his attention and he'd suss out the candidate he'd hope would stick around until the end of the night. Had the exact same thing happened to Annie the food writer, this time last year? My mind was racing over all these possibilities.

"Oh Lily, don't worry about him," consoled The Countess. "See his belly, and his thinning hair? He can land the girls now, but what about in five years' time when the champagne catches up with him? It's not going to be a pretty sight."

We winced. Thank goodness I'd invited her. We went over to the bar area to refill our glasses and we said an enthusiastic "cheers!" to that. On the surface, I might have seemed in agreement with her; however, my eternal hopefulness persisted. At midnight, the guests had to leave the gallery and so a bunch of revelers were going to a nearby bar.

"I'm going to call it a night, and so should you," she advised.

"Maybe I'll go to the bar for just one drink," I said with trepidation, knowing what The Countess would likely reply.

"I don't think it's such a good idea. He barely talked to us all night!"

"Well, he had all of those other guests to mingle with!" I justified rather pathetically.

"Alright, I hope he isn't as stingy with his attention over there. Take care of yourself!" added The Countess. It's good to have friends who look out for you. If this was doomed, I'd have to find out for myself.

Sure enough, over at the bar he was just as busy chatting with other people as he had been at the gallery, even though there were not all that many who'd continued on to the bar with us. I was stuck talking to the older gentleman who'd also been there the night back in May, when this had all begun. Was he the custodian of Tad's rejected conquests?

I finished my drink and got ready to head home with whatever dignity I had left. I didn't even say goodbye to Tad; he'd disappeared to another part of the bar. Besides, judging by his cold shoulder, I doubted he'd miss me.

Crap. I should have been paying more attention to the time! It was 2:00 am and I'd just missed the last *métro*. At this point I exhaled a long, shivering sigh. I wasn't dressed for the recently arrival of chilly mid-November nights. Getting a taxi in Paris at this hour was next to impossible. Any that were circulating were usually already taken by clients who'd started their journey just a tiny bit before. With few other options (this was before the days of Uber), I veered towards the closest *Vélib* bike station. Even if it were freezing, I didn't live too far away by bike and could handle the fifteen-minute ride home.

Double crap. The *Vélib* station was as empty as Tad's emotions. As was the next station. And the one after that. I trembled a few blocks further, finally having luck at the third station, where there was one bike left. By then I'd almost transformed into an icicle, the wintering winds calling for my body and soul to go into hibernation. I slid onto the frosty bike saddle and pushed off towards the traffic lights. When the light turned green, I pedaled like crazy, wanting nothing more than to get home and into my warm bed as quickly as possible.

Triple crap. My frantic pedaling had advanced me about ten feet. No wonder there was just this one bike left at the station: it was defective! I was in some real *mierda*, once again because of Tad. Not seeing much other option I carried on my dismal efforts another block or two at this snail's pace. I ended up abandoning the bike at another station a few blocks away and walking the rest of the way.

In tears.

No, this story wasn't destined to conclude in a happy ending like Dorothy along her Yellow Brick Road. Yet then again, neither do most of the stories those first-class journalists write about in all those fancy newspapers.

Luckily, good friends stand by us even when we don't listen to them and when we do repeatedly stupid things.

"Cheer up, sweetie," soothed The Countess. The weather had stayed brisk, so we decided to meet up over fondue; I thought this would at least warm my spirit a tiny bit. Gooey cheese laced in white wine and dipped in bread... You couldn't get much *heart*ier than that?

"Maybe it was bad karma?" I put forth. "I did kind of stop replying to Benoit's messages and calls."

"You'd only gone out twice," reminded Pussycat, always the pragmatic one. "You did tell him you were busy when he asked you out for a third date, so it's not like you'd ghosted or completely dropped off the face of the earth."

"If it weren't karmic revenge for Benoit, then maybe for the Colombian filmmaker?" slid in Naughty, ever the moralist.

"I did deserve a little chastising for that," I shamefully admitted. I was hoping cleaning my conscience to friends over wine could count as my not-so-holy confession. "Anyway, so Naughty, when are you coming back after the holidays?" At six weeks away, Christmas would be upon us in no time.

"Um, well, I have to tell you guys something…" she cautiously announced. Uh oh, that phrase never meant good news. "I'm not coming back."

About to take a sip, Pussycat plunked down her glass. My fondue stick lost its chunk of bread to the depths of the heated cheese pot. The Countess flagged the waiter to order another bottle of wine. It wasn't for celebrating.

"Girls, don't make this any harder for me," begged Naughty, on the verge of tears. "I've defended and received my Master's, despite my evil supervisor who had it in for me. I've been offered a position at one of the foremost ballet companies in Canada… and I really want to be closer to my boyfriend. It's been a year of long distance now, and it's hard."

Our worst fears were becoming a reality. The Countess wasn't as depressed as we were, she'd only known Naughty for three years. Even though Naughty had been going back and forth between Paris and Toronto for around a year and a half, she was so good at staying in touch and was back here often enough, it didn't seem like she'd ever left. Moving would be a totally different story.

"Have another drink!" she cheered, shakily refilling our glasses. "Besides, we'll see each other soon anyway, at Special Kay's wedding!" Oh yes, next year's weddings were already established. There was my sister's small wedding taking place in March in South Africa. Then Special Kay would be walking down the aisle in April over in her native California.

What was happening to *les filles!* Our little group was either dispersing... or growing up... or both! Here I was, still going around saying I was twenty-six; maybe that's why I had the same old stories on replay over and over again, like Groundhog Day. Was I going to have to 'grow up' as well if I wanted to meet someone serious? Or was it just a matter of taking another approach with the real person I was after?

To: Viktor   Monday, November 21 2010 8:46 PM
Subject: Birthday countdown

Happy early birthday Viktor!

Okay, I might be a month early, but I hope you have a wonderful (and sexy) day! Where are you?? My sister's getting married in South Africa in March... care to be my date? It could be the perfect chance to see your South African cousins, or make a trip back home.

Or, there's always Paris... well, when I'm here.

Kisses,
Lily

P.S. Pre-birthday card attached.

It was time to fan the flames with Viktor. I wasn't just going to poke the coals around. I was going to stoke a fire bigger than the campfire at Walt's golf course, bigger than the one crackling in the grand fireplace at the Count's castle and even bigger than all the cars set on fire by the rioting disgruntled youth in the Paris suburbs, near the Inspector's house. This one would blaze all the way from Paris to Vancouver.

THE POLICE, THE ROLLING STONES AND JACK

From: Jacob   Tuesday, April 12 2011 7:58 AM
Subject: Re: Bonjour!

Oh wow, I still am having a laugh about this time with the
sad, sad man and the amateur police folks! Quite
unbelievable how it all went down, but yes, it certainly
makes for a great story and I am glad to have shared it
with you...

SOMETIMES you just have to live on the edge and go with
the flow, *especially* when things don't go according to plan...

Back in September, one of my old university housemates,
Hannah, let me know she'd be spending a few months in
Spain, starting in November. A bunch of us, who were all
living in the same residence in my first year, got together to
share a big house the following year. Many of them were
studying international relations and were big travelers. In

fact, after graduating, we all scattered across the globe: I ended up in Paris, another went from London to Australia. Hannah herself landed way up in the Canadian Arctic, the reason why we hadn't seen each other since our university days. As such, I was thrilled to get her email suggesting we meet up either in Spain or another European city, while she was over on the continent. A second email from her, letting me know she was all settled in, came right after Tad's bummer of a birthday, and the terribly sad news about Naughty's move back home. Therefore, escaping to Barcelona would be just the spirit-lifting distraction I needed.

One great thing about Paris was that it was easy and cheap to fly to most other European cities, thanks to the arrival of low-cost airlines now cruising the skies. It was completely possible to start your day with a fresh, buttery croissant and a *café crème*, and finish it over some tiramisu and *limoncello*.

I didn't need much convincing to go down to Barcelona. I loved the city so much it was at the top of my list of potential places to move to if I ever decided to leave Paris (yes, right up there with Italy... and Vancouver). An architecturally and culturally rich city, it also benefitted from being on the edge of the Mediterranean Sea, which provided it with a lovely, sunny climate year round.

I'd fallen in love with the city during a three-week partial backpacking trip around the country back when I was waiting for my Work Visa to come through the Scientologists. I say 'partial' backpacking because I'd actually spent half of my time staying with a quirky friend in Malaga and visited the region of Andalusia on day-trips from her place.

Barcelona had been my first stop on this adventure. I'll never forget the first impressions I had of it while wandering around the Gothic Quarter at dawn, trying to find the youth hostel recommended in my guidebook. Despite being incredibly drowsy from a sleepless overnight on the bus, I was enchanted by its narrow, crooked streets, hidden plazas and buildings adorned with climbing vines and hanging laundry—it almost didn't matter that I was completely lost and going in circles—almost (this was pre-smart phones!). I eventually found the hostel, with the help of another lost Canadian backpacker, and we spent the next two days getting lost around the city together.

My return ticket to Paris was also from Barcelona, after sixty hours spent on various buses as I journeyed around the country (and ran into those Argentinians in Madrid who'd tried to get me to have a foursome with them). Entirely exhausted, all I managed to do that last day was crash on the beach next to my backpack, now bonded together by packing tape. It was an unconventional way to form a bond with a place, yet it became a much stronger and longer-lasting bond than the one holding my backpack together.

I returned to the fabulous city a few years later with Special Kay and my good friend Princess Jess, who was over visiting from Vancouver. We had a lively girls' weekend, once again back in the Gothic Quarter and at the beach. This time I was traveling with a much more stylish and sturdier bag.

Not long afterwards, my sister, who was still working as a photographer on cruise ships, was going to make be docking there. So, I met her for a riotous weekend, which got me almost kicked off her ship. The two of us got into a good amount of trouble roaming the bars off Las Ramblas. Let's just blame it on the fact Barcelona was simply a mischievous city!

Well, that it might be, however I wasn't expecting to have a mischievous weekend this time around. Hannah was not coming alone. She was now married and had a small baby. Since Hannah was on maternity leave, they'd jumped at the opportunity to take a sabbatical trip, staying for free at an apartment her husband's family owned in a suburb of Barcelona. This was where we'd be spending most of our time.

Since I'd done a lot of sightseeing on my previous trips, I was more than happy to have a relaxed weekend with them, discovering this other town, dining on tapas, and walking up and down its seaside promenade. Yet, as the day of my flight approached, this little devilish voice persisted in my head: *Hey, wait a second! You're going to one of the world's most fun cities... and you're not going to go out at all?*

That's right, it would certainly be a pity to miss out on the city's lively nightlife. Plus, could I really spend four whole days with a three-month-old baby? While it would definitely be a test to see if I ever wanted children—considering I didn't even have any solid romantic interests at that moment—perhaps such tests could wait! Then, it hit me. I actually did know two other people in Barcelona whom I'd stayed in touch with thanks to Facebook.

So, I sent them each a quick email seeing if they were free on one of the nights I'd be there. The first one I heard back from was Pietro, a friend of one of my best friends in Milan. Unfortunately, he was going to be out of town, so that option was a bust.

Then I received a reply from Sofia, another Italian also from Milan. I'd only met Sofia the previous Christmas, when I was in Milan visiting my Italian family for the holidays. She was a former classmate of a friend of my Italian sister's and she'd joined us for an *aperativo* one evening. With her cheerful personality and broad, genuine smile, we instantly hit it off.

"Let me know when you come to Barcelona!" was her friendly farewell.

Arrivvvvo! I'm coming, Sofia!

From: Sofia   Tuesday, November 30 2010 8:42 PM

Hey there Lily!
Nice to hear from you. I'd love to see you!
On Sunday I'm going to see this really great band, you should totally come!
Let me know!
Sofia

Sunday wasn't exactly the liveliest night of the week, but I jumped at the invitation; at least this way I'd get to go out. Plus, it was the night before I'd be returning to Paris and Sofia kindly offered to let me stay with her. That way, I'd have a little time to amble around the city center the following day before my flight.

Au revoir rainy Paris, *hola* sunny Barcelona! Even in early December, the weather was still pleasant and mild. The first day we did just as I'd imagined: catch up with each other over some *patatas bravas* and *cervezas* while sitting on a terrace facing the beach. In order to do something a little different on the second day, Hannah and her husband suggested going up to Montserrat, a celebrated monastery clinging to a rocky mountain about an hour north. Since they had a car, it would be an easy trip. *¿Por que no?*

I'd seen photos of Montserrat, but they really do not do it justice. As we got closer to the site, we cruised over the crest of a hill and caught first sight of the craggy mountainous fingers rising in the distance, glowing in the late morning sun. Upon seeing this spectacular mountain, like a fist thrusting out of the earth, I could clearly see why it was such a holy place for the Catalan.

We parked at its base and took the funicular up to the top, our awe accelerating as we rose higher and higher. I could imagine that it must be a bit maddening in summer when it was packed with throngs of tourists; however, there were very few other visitors on this late autumn day, allowing the site to regain its intended state of tranquility. After taking in the view and peeking into the church (we'd arrived too late to catch its famous boys choir), we meandered along a mountain path to capture more of the amazing vistas of the valley and other angles of the monastery.

Sunday was another lovely laid-back day, though by the end of the afternoon I'd had my fill of baby time and was eager to have my adult night out in this vibrant city.

Sofia told me to come by her place to drop off my bag before going to the concert together. Arriving at her apartment in a chic district of the city not far from the elegant Passeig de Gràcia avenue, she greeted me with her customary exuberance, making me feel instantly welcome. The quick tour of her apartment ended on her massive terrace, many of its potted flowers still in bloom. If this was Barcelona living, I wanted to move here even more!

The concert was down in the up-and-coming Poble Sec district, a former working-class area now in the process of gentrifying, much like Paris' Belleville neighborhood where I'd attended the African music concert back at the beginning of the year with Antoine and Thomas.

Reaching the area, Sofia and I bunkered down at a bar across from the concert hall for a couple of pre-show drinks (happily, they cost only a fraction of the price they would have in Paris—another reason to love this city!).

"Last night I went up to Zaragoza to see the band's show there!" announced Sofia, brimming with excitement. "It was totally rocked! Then afterwards, we all hung out over some beers! Let's hope we can recreate that tonight. It was so much fun!"

I would gradually learn, as I got to know her better, that Sofia was a big concert-goer, and it wasn't out of the question for her to travel great distances, either across Europe or even over to the States, to see her favorite bands. Tonight's band, Jimmy and the Red Street Rebels, an indie group from New York, had worked their way onto her list. Their music was an eclectic mix of rock, folk and punk. When she'd told me about the concert in her email, I'd thought I'd heard their songs on the French radio station I regularly listened to, but I couldn't say that I really knew any of them well. So, in the days leading up to my departure, I tried to catch up by listening to a few of their albums online to get a better groove on at the concert.

Shortly before show time, we wrapped up our drinks and headed over to the small, historic concert hall. It turned out Sofia's band was opening for another group, the Wicked Waves, a slightly more mainstream group from L.A. who were on tour to promote their latest album. As Sofia had promised, Jimmy and his band were amazing. Jimmy was on fire—during one song, he jumped down from the stage, singing his way through the audience, and in the process igniting the crowd and satisfying its hunger for hard music. The second band had a different style, with a brassy African American lead singer and a more electric sound. It took them a little longer to warm up the crowd, but once they did, they had the audience even more charged than Jimmy had.

Afterwards, Sofia explained that the band usually came out to sign albums and hang with the fans and friends, so we lingered around after the last encores. First to appear was Bob, a guest player who'd been in Jimmy's first punk band back in the '80s. Sofia had befriended him at the previous night's concert and he was thrilled to see her again. Jimmy and the others slowly trickled out, and we congratulated them on the great show and had some laughs with the various band members. As the main band members were still occupied with some fans, Bob suggested we go for some drinks at a bar right across street, different from where Sofia and I had started out, so it would be easy for the others to find us once they'd wrapped up.

The bar was an old school *bodega* style place where both the decor and the bartender looked like they hadn't budged in fifty years. We ordered some *cervezas* and, little by little, the tiny local bar filled with boisterous musicians. Since it was a Sunday, around 1:00 am the unsuspecting grandpa bartender advised us he'd have to close up, so someone suggested heading over to a rock bar that was open all night and wasn't too far to reach on foot. Sofia and I were invited to tag along with the pack. I'd wanted a fun night on the town, and I was getting even more than that! All of the sudden I was hanging out with indie rock stars and their entourage. Not bad at all!

The second bar was like stepping into some sort of musical time warp. Hidden down a quiet alley, it didn't look like much from the outside. However, once inside, we were greeted by blaring classic rock and walls plastered with music memorabilia, everything from signed photos of the Rolling Stones to yellowing posters of AC/DC.

We sipped on more cheap beers and posed for some silly photos with Bob. At some point, Sofia was off talking to

Jimmy and I was chatting to the lead singer of the Wicked Waves about her daughter who wanted to study fashion in Paris. It must have been some time around then that the bassist from her group walked up.

"You live in Paris? That's so cool. We're heading there on Wednesday!" he cheered. "Let's totally meet up! We can put you on the guest list for our show if you want."

The night was just getting better and better! I could use a little more rock and roll in my life; things had gotten way too serious in the past year. We had just exchanged emails, and he started telling me about how much he loved France, when we were interrupted by this Spanish girl. She gave me the most terrifying look of death before yanking the bassist away from our conversation. Geez, what was that all about? She was obviously a tad territorial and, as I'd had very little to do with this other group that night, I pretty much forgot about the incident and went back to goofing off with zany Bob.

I might have brushed off the weird Spanish girl, but I hadn't forgotten about the invitation to the concert. Once back to Paris the next evening—a little groggy from our late night out—I sent the bassist, Jacob, a quick email.

From: Jacob   Tuesday, December 6 2010 2:30 PM
Re: Barcelona - Paris Connection

Lily!

I'm so glad you wrote me - thanks for the message. I will certainly put you on the list for Friday... let me know if you need a +1 or anything. We are actually coming to Paris tomorrow for a Canal Plus TV show and staying in the city.

If you're free at all, I'd love to meet up for a drink or whatever's good. Not sure if I'll have internet access, but... I'll write down your # and try to reach you after the taping.

Was great hanging out in Barcelona - glad you got to see the show and thanks for being so cool at the bar... Ahh, it's very nice to be back in France. Our chef at the venue in Bordeaux tonight made some heavenly things. Santé! J

What an absolute sweetheart! The warmth of his message made my day and it looked like the rocking times from Barcelona would be carrying their beat to Paris. In addition, what was this about Canal Plus, one of France's top TV stations? It appeared that Jacob's band was actually more famous than I'd thought. I loved surprises (well, when they were good ones) and had a feeling the week would have many in store.

Sure enough, the next evening around 9:30 pm I got a message from an unknown number; Jacob was using from his band manager's phone. He'd just finished up and could come meet me in Montmartre. Was I still free? *Mais oui!* Of course! We set a meeting point in front of the *métro* Blanche for 10:00 pm and I excitedly fixed myself up to head down. The last boy I'd met down at this spot was the Dutchie Mario, but luckily he was now long gone from my heart.

There he was, cute Jacob, with sandy blond hair in a hip cut, delicate blue eyes and killer smile, standing under the red glow of the dragonfly-like eyes of the Guimard Art Nouveau *métro* entrance, across from the even sexier Moulin Rouge.

The flame of our evening (and maybe more) was sparked from the start.

We settled in a nearby *café*, ordered a *pichet* of red wine and got to know each other. I was quickly intoxicated by his fun-loving spirit and contagious positivity. Perhaps he'd picked that up when he'd move to sunny California from the chilly Chicago suburbs; regardless of where he got it from, it suited him so well. He was just so laid back and unpretentious, and there was not a drop of a 'I'm an uber-cool rocker' attitude that he could have justifiably had.

He told me tumultuous tales of life on tour, and in turn I recounted stories of Parisian living. Jacob adored Paris so much, and since he was only here for a few days, after drinks I took him on a little stroll around Montmartre, so he could take in more of the city, a casual tour punctuated by laughter and my favorite neighborhood anecdotes. What a lovely night we were having. It was a little sad to say goodbye, when it was time for him to catch the last *métro* back to his hotel… but not before he snuck in a few kisses under the same red glow from a few hours earlier. This was made that much red hotter by Jacob's lips, in essence, completely erasing any bad memories I might have had of that very spot in the past.

I certainly hadn't thought I might meet any romantic interests that night in Barcelona, definitely not one that would follow me to Paris… and one that would have me humming a happy tune again (or was it perhaps a love song?).

"Sounds fun! Sign me up!" replied Pussycat. She was the right wing-woman for this special Friday night. The Countess was more of a champagne lover than a music lover; Naughty was too busy packing (*sniff!*); and besides, Pussycat had the wildest streak of the bunch.

Since this concert was going to be held near my place, I had her over for *apéro* and munchies in preparation for what was forecasting to be a fun night. Plus, I needed to fill her in on the results of the surprising twist to my trip to Barcelona. After a few *verres de vin*, we ventured the five minutes down to the concert venue, a large historic club right across the street from the *métro* station Jacob and I had met at two days prior… and right next to our old hangout O'Hooligan's. In the span of eight years, our Friday nights had gone from flirting our way to the front of the line one venue, to being on the guest list at the other.

There was a pretty good turnout at their concert, probably boosted by their recent TV and radio appearances, making the room nicely full of fans and ambiance. Pussycat and I didn't get a chance to talk to Jacob beforehand, but once on stage he did see we were there since we were up near the front and he shot us a smile whenever he could. Part of Jacob's 'role' in the band seemed to be revving up the crowd, a goal successfully achieved that night leading to two energetic encores.

Jacob came out from back stage afterwards to tell us to stick around. Once the rest of the regular audience had tricked out, he returned with Toni the drummer. The two of them were the 'youngsters' of the group and so inevitably hung out together. They came with a third 'friend' from their dressing room, a bottle of Jack Daniel's. We sat down at a table in the lounge area of the bar and made ourselves some starter drinks with the JD. However, seeing as it was Friday night and this was one of the best areas to go out on the weekend, we didn't want to stay in the confines of the now closed club.

It was around this time the streets under Place Pigalle were becoming the hipster headquarters of Paris, soon nicknamed SoPi, for South Pigalle. Practically every month, a new ultra cool bar replaced one of the seedy escort bars and strip clubs that populated this now dying red light district. A mere few weeks back, I'd gone to a Halloween party at the latest hotspot, a club in the former private mansion of composer George Bizet. Named after his best-known operatic masterpiece, the interior of the club was magnificently decorated with plush armchairs, sparkling chandeliers and other antiques evocative of the époque when the composer lived here. It felt like we were guests at a private party he was hosting—only Bizet had been replaced by a hip DJ, and top hats by tattoos. I suggested we try to get in there first; I figured it would impress our special out-of-towners. So, we slid the bottle of JD into Pussycat's rather large purse and off we went.

Reaching the venue, Jacob and Toni managed to get us past the two beastly bouncers with the convincing line in English of "Hey man, we're in the band that just played up the road." We ordered a Coke, requested an empty glass, found a corner table to perch ourselves on and discretely mixed in some whiskey from our traveling 'mini-bar' (aka Pussycat's purse). I knew Toni, an attractive young Asian American, had his eye on Pussycat, but since she'd recently met a more serious romantic contender (yes, her too!), I knew she wouldn't be swayed. It didn't really matter since we were having a fun time all together.

We hung out there for a little while, but when the music stagnated, we decided to see what other fun we could find in the area. A short giggly stumble out the door and we crashed into a lively bunch of smokers, hanging out in front Chez Mimi, a former underground lesbian club turned hipster-haven. After a quick chat, our new 'friends' were were making their way inside the cool club, so we tagged along.

Oh boy, those were narrow, winding steps down to the basement club level, made all the more dangerous because of the JD. We hit the dance floor straight away, but this is when the JD hit Pussycat, and hard. As she'd been carrying it in her purse, she'd gotten a little friendlier with JD than the rest of us and was looking to take him to bed with her, by passing out on one of the lounge's sofas. Being of sounder mind, although only slightly, I escorted her up to the main street to find her in a taxi home. Mission accomplished and returning to Chez Mimi, I found Jacob and Toni hanging outside the club with some freshly-made friends. I guess being on the road so much they were used to chatting with complete strangers. At some point, when Toni looked in good company with his new buddies, Jacob and I drifted away on our own…

From: Jacob   Saturday, December 10 2010 8:31 PM
Re: It's meeee

Hey Lily!

What a randomly beautiful and fantastic night in Paris we had! I'm so glad you came to the show, and thanks for bringing Pussycat - what a riot that she got so unbelievably twisted… and I just had a really lovely time hanging with you.

I managed to take an hour nap before soundcheck today - thankfully, since three hours or so of sleep is not nearly enough for the amount of energy I will be required to expend on stage tonight…

It was such a beautiful morning in Paris - it was really a shame to leave. I hope you had a great day and were able to accomplish what you needed! I'm so jealous of where you live!! Just think - collectively, we live in two of the hippest neighborhoods in the world ;)

Time to rest before tonight's show! Talk to you soon…
xoxo
J

Jacob was such a sweetie. We'd had a fabulously fun night, he'd (almost) made me forget all about the whole Tad fiasco. But I knew The Countess wouldn't.

"So, any news from Mr. Champagne Belly?" she coyly fished.

"Um, ah, nope. But I did get a nice email from Jacob!" She rolled her eyes; she was not a big fan of my rebellious rocker, rather unfairly since she'd never met him. I could just imagine her disapproving thoughts.

"It's not like Tad was worth trying to salvage anyway! He's certainly moved on to the next girl on his email list!" I defended. Both men traveled the world: one drank champagne, the other cheap beer and whiskey, but at least one actually stayed in touch regularly.

"Yah, but this 'dude' lives in California," she added in her best attempt at an American accent.

"Well, that's exactly where we'll be in a few months!" reminded Naughty, assumedly to change the subject. I really hoped to see him again, and if not in Paris, I might be lucky enough to catch him when we were in Cali for Special Kay's wedding.

Despite the great time Jacob and I had, from the start I did realize there was virtually no way anything would really come of our chance encounter and that we might not even see each other ever again. I didn't think he was my soul mate (a feeling which was evidently mutual), yet we had good chemistry and I'd decided to just go with this unforeseen flow, to simply take things for what they were and enjoy the fleeting moments. This was something I was especially welcome to doing due to the romantic doldrums I'd fallen into just before meeting him. But, I knew it was merely a distraction, an escape from actually trying to find somebody real... an excuse to not give up on waiting for Viktor.

Actually, I had to admit Viktor had been on my mind more these days. It was just a week away from his birthday. Since he'd turned down my invitation to attend my sister's wedding, I was certainly less inspired to send him an updated birthday card, one which could contain an invitation to join me in California; L.A. was at least closer to him, but I was now leaning more and more against bothering with it. How many times could I try with him? We hadn't seen each other in ten years; what if he was no longer the cute, fun Viktor I'd remembered? I decided I'd stick to my distraction for the time being, but before I could do that, we were about to go into mourning.

The time had come. It was a rare occasion when we'd meet up at Naughty's, mainly because she kept hopping around the city to different sublets due to all the traveling back and forth she'd been doing this past year or so. In her small *chambre de bonne* studio apartment, under the rooftops of the somewhat edgy 17th district, bordering picture-perfect Montmartre, we were having our last bottle of Domaine de Valentin together. Sure, there would be other clanking of glasses to be had with Naughty, but these would be in California, Toronto, the English countryside or back here in Paris on what we'd hoped would be frequent visits from her. However, on a daily basis, how would we survive without her? Would we have to double our dose of Valentin?

"Cheers!" we said in unison, hoping the glow of the candles reflecting off our glasses would be confused as the cause of our glossy, teary eyes.

"May the new year bring us happiness, lots of girls' get-togethers... and getting together with the right boys!" she attempted, trying to add some positivity to the gloomy undertone of our supposed 'celebration.' I wasn't sure if those were the 'right' things to wish for us, especially the latter. She appeared to be on the right track for that; Special Kay was getting married; Pussycat was getting more serious with her new British beau; and The Countess wasn't seeking to get tied down—she was adequately amused with getting her ex-*amant* to take her out to the city's best restaurants at the snap of her elegant fingers. Perhaps Santa would bring me a cute Southern African in his sack of toys... or, I'd certainly settle for quick return of a sunny-spirited American.

It was looking like I might get my wish after all, since Jacob hadn't drop off the face of my earth. We really did 'talk to each other soon' via newsy updates on our lives, me from grey, wintery Montmartre and him from balmy Venice Beach. Early on in his messages he said the band would most likely be coming back to Europe for a longer tour in March and April. This brightened my prospects for a blossoming spring romance, especially if I could see him a few times during his return. But, the next friendly email in my inbox was not from cheerful Jacob...

FROM: Viktor   Wednesday, March 23 2011 9:10 PM
Re: re: your invitation
Hey Lily,
How are you? I am in Japan at the moment in the beautiful small city of Kyoto. I have been cycling for

almost 3,000 kms this year. I think by now you must
be back from South Africa? How was it?

I just wanted to let you know that I was thinking of you
perhaps it was all these Eiffel Tower look-alikes that
they seem to have here in Japan, or perhaps the
thought of the birthday card you sent?

With love, Viktor

Japan? What the heck was he doing in Japan? My
excitement upon seeing his name in my inbox instantly
transformed into sadness, fury and exasperation all rolled
into one giant *grrrr*. It wasn't that I had any problem with
Japan per say… and Kyoto was probably a fabulous place.
The point was that he'd gone there right at the same time as
I'd invited him to come to my sister's wedding with me. Sure,
they were very different trips and circumstances, but if he was
going to take a holiday, why didn't he want to take it with
me? Or at the very least come and see the darn Eiffel Tower
in person, if he really wanted to see it? Plus, he said he 'was
thinking of me.' Was it just a passing thought now and then,
or was he inviting me to probe a little deeper into what
'thinking of me' actually meant? How was my holiday? It
would have been wonderful had he been there with me…

Well, actually the trip to celebrate my sister's union to her
long-term South African boyfriend was very special. That is,
once my sister's panic over her dress not fitting right
dissolved. She and her now husband exchanged their vows in
an unconventional ceremony held on their favorite beach and
attended by thirty of their close local friends, his immediate
family and with my mom and I representing my sister's side.

For someone who didn't think I'd ever get married—*especially* after the horrible incident I'd endured at the last wedding I'd attended up in England—I might be willing to concede to this sort of laid back, eccentric ceremony... that is if I ever found someone I'd consider marrying (or who would marry me!). My sister had tried matching me up with the only other 'single' person at the event. Okay, he was a really hot underwear-model-type friend of my new brother-in-law, so this might have seemed a tempting prospect. I just wasn't into passing hook-ups and had no plans to move to South Africa, despite its natural and *masculine* beauty (underwear model-esque or not!). It was just a shame he hadn't been the other African I had my virtual eye on.

The frustrations about Viktor were soon swept away by a good news email from Jacob:

> From: Jacob   Friday, March 25 2011 9:25 PM
> Subject: Re: Bonjour!
>
> Lily! A quick heads up that I'm coming to Paris today! We land Saturday morning...
> Hope to see you!!

I was absolutely thrilled at the prospect of seeing him and knew he'd boost my morale, but there was a stumbling block in our plans, my mom was in town. Poor Mom, during the few trips she'd made to Paris, some mischief always arose, like the 'accidental' all-nighter my sister and I pulled with the adorable Keanu Reeves look-a-like we'd run into on her previous trip here. There was no way I could do a repeat this time around! While I'd come back from the wedding trip two weeks ago, she'd stayed on to spend more time with my sister. She'd just arrived in Paris the night before Jacob's return and was exhausted from the long flight. Therefore, she gave me her grace to go out, with my hand-on-heart promise to come home at a decent hour (one much before dawn).

I tucked mom into bed around 10:00 pm and cruised over to meet Jacob. He was already with other friends of his over by the Canal Saint Martin, its lively cafés overflowing with Friday night revelers. It was so nice to see joyful Jacob. We had some laughs over a few *pichets* of wine with his buddies, then the two of us took a stroll along the glimmering canal, possibly one of the most romantic places in the city. I couldn't help thinking, as we walked hand-in-hand along the water, with him pulling me in closer for a tender kiss now and then, that I wished there wasn't an ocean—and then the whole width of a continent—that separated us.

From: Jacob Thursday, March 31 2011 7:41 PM
Subject: Re: Bonjour!

Hey hey!

Just got back into France! Sorry, we had really dodgy web connects in the UK, just saw your message. I should totally be able to put you on a list for the Paris show - should I do a plus one in case you want to bring a friend?

I'm so glad you came out the other night on such short notice and with your mom in town... It was fun!

I believe we get in town early, around 12:00 for soundcheck, so I will probably have some time before the show - maybe you'd like to have dinner or something?

Lemme know if you have time... I'll try to call you from
Matthieu's phone after soundcheck.
Bisous bisous

See you again very soon :)
xoxo J

This next time I had a little advance notice of Jacob's
arrival, but I was beginning to recognize a pattern with him,
which generally involved spontaneity and surprises.

First off, Jacob surprised me by finishing up even earlier
than expected. I'd assumed that he might have a quick hour
or two around 5:30 pm, but I received a text message saying
he could meet me an hour and a half earlier. Slipping out of
work a touch early wouldn't really hurt—I put in more than
my fair share of overtime. The problem was that I'd planned
to go home before the concert to change, and was currently
wearing a nice spring dress to match the increasingly lovely
seasonal weather... not exactly concert apparel. Still, I went
to meet him, intending to zip home before the show.

We rendezvoused not far from my office, parking
ourselves on the sunniest terrace in the busy Les Halles area.
He devoured the wine and cheese we ordered, and I his
exciting stories from the road. We were having such a nice
time that we didn't noticed the passing hours, and soon Jacob
had to get back to the concert hall over near Place de la
République.

"Just come straight there with me now!" he urged with his
trademark broad smile. Never one to turn down a fun offer, I

popped into the clothing shop across the square from where we were sitting and quickly chose a better concert outfit (a black top and skirt), then texted Pussycat to see if she could lend me some more appropriate shoes since she would once again be my date. I changed in the concert hall bathroom and stuffed my dress in my bag. *Voilà!* I was magically transformed into a little rocker girl... or at least something cooler than a little office girl.

The mid-sized concert hall was packed and the atmosphere abuzz with their high-energy fans; I was starting to get to know their songs better so I was blending right in with the best of them. After the concert, our boisterous group took over the bar next door. When it eventually closed up around 1:00 am, we decided to keep the festivities going on nearby rue Oberkampf. It was gradually losing its hip area status to SoPi, but its strip of late-night bars would suit our purposes.

Pussycat went home at that point; she was trying to steer clear of 'Jack' this time, something Jacob wouldn't let her live down in a gentle, teasing way. Tonight would not be as riotous as usual because they had to leave at 7:00 am the next morning, but some more 'adventure' was yet to play out in our cards. Around 2:30 am we headed back to their hotel, located on a small street behind the concert venue. Dark and rather dingy, it didn't really seem an acceptable place to put up international performers, but it must have been chosen for its proximity to the concert hall.

When we arrived, Jacob and Toni had to get their keys from reception, a common practice in France. However, the disgruntled night watchman was not at all receptive about granting access to a third guest.

"But there's even a second bed in my room!" protested Jacob.

"Ze reservation is for one people," the watchman retorted in bad English. He wouldn't budge.

"Come on man; what's the big deal?" added Jacob, who started to walk me off to the elevator, angering Monsieur Grumpy even more.

"Maybe I can just pay a supplement for an additional person if that's the problem?" I suggested timidly. Neither seemed interested in this possibly solution, both more stubborn than the other. More nasty words that neither could understand were exchanged leading to an indignant Jacob marching me off towards his room, he broke into giggles as soon as we were in the elevator. He did not take *non* very well.

Up in his room, the phone rang. The night watchman was not going to give up; in return Jacob silenced his threats of calling the police by hanging up and leaving the phone off the receiver. For him, it was settled, and he turned his attention to what interested him more: me, and removing the red panties I was wearing.

Around twenty minutes later, there was knocking at the door.

"C'est la Police," informed the knocker. *Merde!* That tough watchman was true to his word. I froze in panic; however, Jacob remained as cool as a cucumber. There was no messing with him.

I tiptoed off to the bathroom and Jacob, refusing to acknowledge he understood any French whatsoever, opened the door a crack and twirled the French beat cops around with his foreign words and fake incomprehension.

"What are you talking about? There's no girl in here," he adamantly denied. Before long, he had their heads spinning; their English was way too mediocre to challenge his linguistic tactics. Obviously, the door wasn't open enough to see my red underwear located on the ground nearby. It wasn't like they had a warrant, so there wasn't really much they could do, and Jacob must have realized that. Even though the police eventually left—claiming they'd be back in the 'morning' to retain his passport—the watchman wasn't going to give up and went back to insistently calling the room (Jacob must have put the phone back on the hook). I wasn't as stubborn as him, compromising with the grouch, with payment for an extra person. He got his twenty-five extra Euros, I got a receipt, and Jacob got to keep me (for a little longer)… and his passport.

It was sad to say goodbye to Jacob at 7:00 am the next morning, I didn't know when I'd see my California cutie again. After waving after their vanishing tour bus I made my way to the *métro*. I was rarely out in the streets of Paris so early in the morning. Climbing the steps out of my station, I was struck by the golden glow bathing Place des Abbesses, announcing yet another beautiful spring day. The peace reigning over the cobbled square was only interrupted by a passing jogger or the clank of a waiter setting up the tables and chairs on an outdoor café terrace. It was times like this that I wondered if I could I ever leave my cherished Paris. I almost wanted to sit down at one of those freshly lain chairs and savor the moment over *un petit café*, but the idea, and my minute of reflection, quickly vanished when I realized how disastrous I must have looked. Instead, I crept back to my place, hoping to avoid any of my crotchety old neighbors on this walk of rock'n'roll shame. Safe and sound in front of my apartment door, I rustled through my bag for my keys. Hey, where was the dress I'd been wearing before the concert? Looked like the night watchmen would end up with another souvenir of his rocky (in more ways than one) night!

From: Jacob   Tuesday, April 12 2011 7:58 AM
Subject: Re: Bonjour!

Lily!

Oh wow, I still am having a laugh about this time with the sad, sad man and the amateur police folks! Quite unbelievable how it all went down, but yes, it certainly makes for a great story and I am glad to have shared it with you...

Greece was amazing! Great shows, lovely people, crazy good food, beautiful scenery, etc. Hope your week is off to a good start. We head to Amsterdam today! I'm sure we'll find plenty of trouble to get into :) hopefully no police will be involved...

Hugs- J

There seemed to always be a crazy adventure with Jacob. Was that only what it would ever be?

The San Diego International Airport must be one of the scariest in the world to fly into. I'd been on dozens and dozens of planes and wasn't normally afraid of flying, however, I couldn't help but tighten my grip on my arm rest. I gaped out the window in horror as we glided amidst the city's high-rises, finally coming to a skidding halt right at the ocean's edge. I'd been ready to go into the brace position, or should I have been bracing myself instead, for yet another wedding?

No inappropriate advances or pawning me off onto single friends at this one. Unfortunately, Jacob was still in Europe, so I couldn't convince him to come down as my date. This was probably a good thing, who knows what kind of trouble he might have been instigated. The only dangerous incidents on the trip were the romantic battles playing out in my mind.

Special Kay was the first of the Paris girls to get married— the first of my last wave of friend weddings. Was it the end of the era or merely the happy transition to something else? I still wasn't sure, but it was definitely a quandary that hung over me as Naughty, Pussycat and I wiggled into our bridesmaid's dresses in the Sunday school room of Kay's parish church, close to her small town in the Laguna foothills. Kay was glowing and serenely prepared to embark on this new life journey, to be traveled by two. We toasted to their happiness with crisp Californian 'champagne' and kept the sleepy country folk guests up past their 10:00 pm bedtime.

Here I was, a three-hour flight away from Viktor. Grumbling to myself, I was regretting not having squeeze in a few days up in Vancouver since I was so close. That said, I'd just taken two weeks of holiday down in South Africa the previous month. France does have generous holiday time, but I was working for Americans and was already pushing it with this trip so soon after the last. Instead, I was planning on going over to see my Mom over on the West Coast in the fall. This time I wasn't going to let Viktor slip out of my hands; I'd check my travel dates with him prior to booking my flight. Then I would finally know if I should be holding out for him any longer or if I should 'woman up' and officially move on. Regardless of my desire for advance planning, the Parisian love vibes had other, more imminent things in store for me.

From: Jacob   Friday, April 29 2011 11:40 PM
Subject: Re: Bonjour!

Lily!!

What's happening? Have you already gone to California? I'm sure you have, but are you back?

We have just absolutely been on a whirlwind around Europe, the past few weeks had gone by so fast! After Amsterdam we tackled most of Germany, and then hit Budapest and Slovenia before going through Italy for a week or so. We actually just enjoyed two days off with hotels right on the beach in Italy, on the Mediterranean near the Cinque Terre (amazing!). And now, unbelievably, we have only six shows to go.

I hope your trip was amazing, and that you had good weather and Cali treated you right! Can't wait to hear about it...

Hugs and bisous,
J

At least *someone* wanted to stay in contact with me. I put my fretting about weddings and tepid Africans on the back burner and enjoyed the warmth of Jacob's sunny disposition.

From: Jacob   Saturday, May 7 2011 8:54 PM
Subject: Re: Bonjour!

Hey hey Lily!
And how are you?! I miss Paris so much!

It's crazy - I feel like I just got here, but our summer touring season is just about to start. We leave tomorrow for a two-week run in the US and Canada (YES!) and then back for just a few days before blasting off to Europe for a long ass time. I think we'll be staying in Orleans for a while and going out to do festivals on the weekends, and there's talk of us having an apartment in Brussels at some point, too.

I look forward to seeing you somewhere down the line ;)
All the best,
xo J

I might have missed seeing him again the next time around, luckily, it sounded like he'd be back in the summer. It wasn't like I would be waiting around for him, but once again he provided a handy distraction from trying to find some spring romance flowers to pick back in Paris. I went about my other life priorities like sipping rosé at café terraces around the city with The Countess and Pussycat.

From: Tad   Tuesday, May 10 2011 6:29 PM
Subject: Bulles!

My Fellow Media Hacks and Flacks and Special Guests:

It's been a year since all of us got together. We're way
overdue. Let's get ruined on champagne on Wednesday at
Bubbles (a fairly new Champagne bar near Bastille) and
discuss lofty ideas: Ratko Mladic's haircut, best Yemeni
beach clubs, favorite moments in DNA evidence, and
other lofty subjects.

Who's in? Let me know!
Look forward to seeing you all!

Tad

Sigh! I'd just managed to forget about that whole debacle,
sealing it in a mental box marked 'Dangerous: Explosive
Material. Do Not Reopen.' I hadn't heard from him since the
last party invite back in November. I was a bit surprised to
still be on his invite list; obviously he really never cleaned it
up or he merely like to test which girls withstood his non-
committal behavior. I just couldn't resist forwarding the
message to The Countess:

THE COUNTESS [05/10/11 7:15 PM]
But remember we decided that he was
a BAD person... do you think the
champagne will be free?!

LILY LA TIGRESSE [05/10/11 8:07 PM]
I KNOW he is definitely a BAD person, it
was just funny to receive his message. You
told me to send news when/if I heard from
him again. I doubt the bulles will be free or
else I'd actually consider going. I wasn't
even going to reply!

THE COUNTESS [05/10/11 8:20 PM]
If the bulles were free you would have to go
and only talk to young handsome men with
full heads of hair and trim waistlines!!
Have a fun Saturday xx

Now this is what friends are for. Especially in my case, considering I can make such dodgy decisions, it's valuable to have someone to talk—or *type*—some sense into you. I really, really wasn't intending to go to the event, even if it would probably feature dateable young handsome men with full heads of hair and trim waistlines, I would dream of other international candidates.

VOULEZ-VOUS COUCHER AVEC
NOUS *CE SOIR?*

THOMAS 3/08/2011 10:59 PM
Ok, but if you want to meet up at your
place after midnight for an intellectual...
and sensuellllle visit... or else on
Sunday? Kisses

I WAS PLANNING on coasting nonchalantly through the summer. I was more than content with a few fun visits from Jacob while I awaited my much anticipated and overdue reunion with Viktor scheduled for the autumn. However, the troublesome, amorous encrgy of Paris (and a few other destinations) had other plans for me...

Before anything else though, I needed to lay the terrain for an encounter with Viktor. I would need to ensure he'd actually be in town for the dates I was planning to go, and I also needed to stoke the romantic fires to make sure some sort of result came of the visit, positive or not.

> From: Viktor   Wednesday, June 22 2011 6:55 AM
> Subject: Re: Happy Summer!
>
> Lily,
>
> Wow, I have to say that it took more than several moments for me to be able to peel my eyes off my screen. What a wonderful sight to behold, and thank you for brightening up my winter! You have more than my curiosity piqued.
>
> Do you remember that art project you did with a full body cutout? I don't remember what happened with that in the end.
>
> Well, I hope the summer gets suitably warmer. Perhaps even warm enough to encourage you to lose a few more pieces of clothing ;) The ante has been upped, so I shall have to figure out an appropriate response…
>
> Xoxo Viktor

Ah ha! My special message certainly caused the temperature to rise! I'd used the convenient premise of the start of summer to reach out with a slightly racy 'seasonal' greeting aimed as a starting point for bringing up my planned visit to Vancouver. He even had fond memories of my art created a decade ago. Perhaps I did hold a special place in his mind (and heart)? So proud of getting a reaction out of him, I didn't immediately notice the peculiar line about brightening up his winter? Geez, Vancouver's unique micro-climate usually meant its winters weren't very cold like the rest of Canada. Besides, it should definitely have been over by June.

Before I could even bring up this quizzical point in a follow-up email, I received a new message from him:

From: Viktor   Thursday, June 23 2011 5:42 PM
Subject: Re: Happy Summer!

Lily,
From the mist you can see in the distance, you can see it is chilly on the Omaruru River. About five degrees I think. In some ways am embarrassed to share that just posing for this got me worked up enough to have to share a small part of me with that beautiful river scene. Being in nature has always had that effect on me - I don't know what it is.

I would love to hear more about your book - what is it about?

Hope to see more soon... much more. :)
Viktor

The Omaruru? That definitely didn't sound like it could be the name of a Canadian river. Well, that explained his 'winter.' He was down in Africa and their winter was just beginning! If it hadn't been for his attachment, I might have been infuriated—once again not bothering to stop off in Europe on his way to Africa (or not that I knew of…).

Now, it was my turn to 'wow' and with much more reason than the PG-13 photo I'd sent him! His email describes the setting very well; there he was again, similar to his photo sent from Malaysia, standing around twenty feet away and with his back to the camera, showing off all of his very fit body. Looks like all that biking in Japan had paid off!

I had squeezed into my message that I was finally almost finished writing my first book; little did he know he would have a prominent role in the second (nor did I at the time), but at that very moment, nothing was certain. Most importantly, if he really had feelings for me and was still as timid to try anything as he was ten years ago, when we'd last seen each other. Hopefully I'd finally get to the bottom of things in a few months' time.

Meanwhile, a bubbly message saved me from being too depressed.

> From: Jacob   Tuesday, July 6 2011 10:34 PM
> Subject: Re: Bonjour!
>
> Yoohoo Lily,
>
> How are you? I hope your summer is off to a good start. I'm in France! Got in yesterday and now we're chillin way down south in St Martin de Crau getting ready to play our first festival of the summer!
>
> There's a good chance I'll be coming to Paris next week - Toni and I want to check out the Bastille Day festivities, and our other option is staying in Orleans, which tends to get a bit boring.
> I hope you're well! Send me your number again, and I'll get in touch if we come to the city :)
>
> xx Jacob

Bastille Day was one of the highlights of my annual social calendar, just after the wine fair (hopefully I wouldn't meet any more great grandpas at the fair in the future, though!). If you ask a French person what they are doing for 'Bastille Day,' they'll just give you a puzzled look like you'd asked them if they liked *baguettes*. They refer to it either as *La Fête Nationale* or just '*le 13 juillet / le 14 juillet*' (the National Day, or the 13th/14th of July). Why the 13th? Because that's when *la fête* truly begins, possibly because it was on the night of the 13th to the 14th of July 1789 that the Bastille prison was stormed, the official marker of the beginning of the French Revolution... or potentially for the less patriotic reason that the 14th is a public holiday allowing *les fêtards* to nurse their hangovers. Leave it to the French to plan a good party! But, that's not where the clever planning ends.

The highlights of these parties include champagne, cheesy bands, and pole-dancing firemen. No, the country's Chippendales do no donate their services for the night; much better, these dancing firemen are *real* since the official festivities, called *les Bals des Pompiers*, are held at fire stations across the country. All proceeds from the parties go towards the running of the fire halls, so sipping away on champagne and ogling the staff was actually a charitable activity. The ambience at these balls tends to start out 'family-friendly,' but some halls can get quite wild, like at the one in the 1st arrondissement where a techno party took place in a back room. Here's where you were most likely to feast your eyes on the pole dancing firemen... however, there are plenty of them milling about at any of the balls, just maybe not stripped down to their undies.

We always had a blast at the firemen's balls (*at* not *with*!). The previous year, The Countess and I attended our our second favorite ball, held at the fire hall on the Canal Saint Martin. She was feeling particularly feisty and dared me to the following challenge: acquire a token from a fireman, such as a button from their jacket, with bonus points awarded for getting ahold of his hat or stripe ranks. Not one to shy away from challenges, I kept on the lookout for any opportunities to talk to passing firemen.

Things were not looking so promising and just when I was about to give up, a fireman started chatting me up. After some minor small talk, out of nowhere he kissed me! Maybe my lips appeared to be burning and he felt professionally compelled to put them out? The Countess had to accept defeat, as I'd definitely won, I'd even been given his phone number. Moreover, this was right after I'd escaped from Inspector Cluzot... pursuing a man in uniform seriously was absolutely not on my dating agenda!

Back to this year and the reason I would *not* be seeking out any firemen to flirt with. Jacob was reliable—up to a point. He said he'd be coming, gave me a week's advance notice, but then the details of when and where we'd meet up remained rather vague. I definitely wanted to see him, but wasn't going to be waiting around at home for his call that night. Pussycat was out of town, so I wrangled The Countess into coming out with me. The plan was to start at a pre-Firemen's ball party I'd been invited to by a fun gay friend, Luke. He just so happened to live right around the corner from the previously mentioned ball in the 1st district, so we'd make our way there after a few glasses (or bottles) of rosé. I'd keep an eye on my phone for news from Jacob and adjust accordingly.

There was one slight hiccup—or rather *sneeze*—in my plan for the evening: I seemed to be coming down with the flu, or tonsillitis, or something unpleasant like that. I didn't fall ill very often and I wasn't going to let whatever I'd caught keep me bedridden on this most festive night of the summer. So, I chugged a mug of Fervex (a strong French cold and flu drink) before going down to Luke's, and put another pack in my purse for later.

The ambiance was lively and the rosé abundantly poured in Luke's small but very central studio apartment, currently packed with eight eager revelers. At 9:00 pm we could hear the music start up since we were so close to the fire station. After the remaining wine bottles were emptied a short while later, we made our way to *le bal*, hoping to arrive before the line got too long. Our timing was right, and as soon as we gave our donation at the entrance, Luke bee-lined us straight through the crowd to the back room where the underwear-clad pole-dancing firemen would be. We ordered a bottle of their bubbly and were soon hypnotized by the bodacious *pompiers* in their tight briefs. Despite the blaring music and bone-shaking beats, I somehow heard (or maybe felt) my phone buzzing with a new message:

UNKNOWN NUMBER [07/13/11 11:30 PM]
Hey Lils, we're heading to le bal along
the canal, meet you there? - J

"Countess! He's going to the station from last year! Are you still game?" I shouted over the booming music.

"Only if you let me win the fireman this time!" she shouted back. "But I take it that as you're meeting up your band guy, I'll win by default! Either way, I'll win by finally getting to meet this Jacob guy."

Before we left for the second ball, I poured my backup packet of Fervex into a glass of water, which I chased with the rest of my champagne; hoping it would keep my cold at bay.

It didn't take us long to reach the other ball, however, as we rounded the corner towards it, we realized we weren't the only ones who'd arrived late. A colossal line zigzagged between the fire hall and the canal. It looked like it could take an hour to get in! As we got closer, we noticed that there seemed to be two security check lines, so we naturally jumped in the shorter of the two and eventually made it inside.

LILY LA TIGRESSE [07/14/11 12:45 AM]
We're by the bathroom

I sent Jacob a report, and we waited around there for a while. Something seemed off, though I couldn't put my finger on it...

UNKNOWN NUMBER [07/14/11 12:53 AM]
Okay, I'm here too, I don't see you

I scanned my surroundings and couldn't see him anywhere in sight. In fact, I wasn't seeing much of anything very clearly. Yes, this was the bathroom; I could see the little man/woman signs... but wait a second, were the stick-figures dancing together? My head was also swinging and it didn't seem to be from disco lights nor from the champagne.

I tried to focus. Hey, where were the firemen? Where was the band blasting '80s cover songs?

Damn! We finally understood we were at the bar *next door* to the firehouse, not at the ball itself. That's why the line hadn't been as bad! So out we went and got into the other line, which seemed even longer than before (if that was even possible), making conditions atrocious. We were pushed, shoved and groped by drunken or sleazy guys, who were trying to profit from our forced confinement in line.

"Hey Countess, now I remember where those bathrooms at the firehouse are... they are over on the other side. Maybe there's another entrance over there?" I'd had an epiphany, which was a miracle considering the fogginess clouding my brain, caused by a toxic mix of rosé, champagne, loud music... and Fervex. That's what had put me over the edge— cold meds and booze are not meant to go to the *Bal des Pompiers* together.

Making our way all around to the other side (in my case, swerving my way there), we found... a large chain-link barrier through which I could see the meeting point with Jacob, about forty feet away. So close yet completely out of reach. We couldn't storm this Bastille; we were not valiant revolutionaries. I tried his friend's phone again and again, but to no avail. They'd likely gone back inside to enjoy the fun and couldn't hear it with all the loud music, or simply ignored it as I was starting to make no sense at all with my Fervex-infused dialect. Collapsing in despair, The Countess eventually packed me up in a cab and sent me home. Alas, neither of us won our sought-after prize that night.

The Fervex continued to fail on me, all the way through to the end of the box when, a few days later, I finally dragged myself and my scratchy throat to the doctor to get some medication for my... bronchitis.

Off Jacob went to play at some of Europe's biggest music festivals and I was stuck in Paris on antibiotics, dopily wondering if I'd get a chance to see him again on this trip or not. Instead of cruising through summer, my ride was turning into a sad romantic flop. Woe was entirely me (and my poor throat).

Romantic pursuits were far from my mind as August rolled around a few weeks later. It was the quietest month in Paris, with so many of its residents fleeing the city on lengthy holiday, which could last the whole four weeks. The city virtually becomes a ghost town. While some love the city when it's so quiet, the tranquility depressed me; it was like its vibrant energy I so adored, had been completely drained. However, since I'd already used up so many holiday days with my trips to South Africa and California, it looked like I'd have to pretty much stick it out this year. Well, there would always be a nice bottle of rosé to keep me company.

THOMAS [08/03/2011 4:21 PM]
Salut Lily, I hope you're doing well. It's
been a while! Do you want to meet
Antoine and me tomorrow?
Bises Thomas

Wow, it looked like I might have some company after all. What a surprise to hear from Thomas, it had been quite some time indeed. After our chilly evening going to the African concert with Antoine back at the beginning of last year, Thomas sent me a handful of text messages trying to get me to meet him for a drink, movie, Turkish coffee, Japanese tea ceremony... but I never seemed 'available.' I just knew I wasn't really into him and didn't want to get his hopes up, though I did feel a little bad that I'd sort of brushed him off. From the chipper tone of his message, he didn't seem too bothered.

THOMAS [08/03/2011 5:38 PM]
I'm supposed to meet Antoine at
Luxembourg, but I don't know what
we're doing yet! Maybe a cafe-concert!
I'll let you know! Bises Thomas

Of course, I ran the risk of him (or both of them) flirting with me... and trying who knows what. But I thought I could easily handle them. I was looking forward to doing something a little different and who knows: maybe Antoine would bring along the 'Ryan Gosling' whom I was dreaming of the last time.

THOMAS [08/03/2011 4:18 PM]
Salut Lily, so we're meeting up at Lux
at 9 PM in front of the RER station.
Looking forward to seeing you!

Nine?! Even if it was a Friday night, that was quite late and wasn't really *apéro* time nor dinner. With this tardy rendezvous time, I'd go home after work, chill out for a bit, then trek down to the station at Luxembourg, just outside the pretty park bearing the same name. Relaxing in the gardens would not be an option for this little get together, like we'd done in the past. Even if Antoine brought along Ryan… or Adrien it would still be closed. Though central, this part of town was complicated to get to from my neck of the woods. After these grumblings, I told myself to stop my bemoaning and just be grateful; with all of my usual friends away that week, I know this may be the only invitation I'd have to go out for a while.

ALAIN [08/03/2011 4:30 PM]
Hey there, free tonight? I'm having
a few people over for some rosé

What was this? A second invitation? If the rest of my month of August was going to be like this, it actually wouldn't turn out all that bad! Alain, huh? This was the first time he'd actually invited me out directly to do something…

I'd know him for the past few years. He was a friend of Mademoiselle Sécret and we'd chat with each other occasionally at parties. Tall, svelte and rather handsome, Alain was a mid-thirties French TV reporter and host, specializing in alternative religions of the world (*noooo*, not like Scientology!). He spent half the year with his 'spiritual advisor' in Bali (in the days before *Eat Pray Love*) and the rest either in Paris or off interviewing gurus in India or medicine men in the Amazon. With my eccentric upbringing, I couldn't help be intrigued by his spiritual quests... almost as much as I was with his gorgeous green eyes.

I had never even bothered flirting with him because, for four years, he'd been dating a yoga instructor who was off-the-wall, but gorgeous in the 'natural I don't have to wear make-up kind of way'; she also looked like she could kill you with her warrior position for merely laughing at one of his jokes. So, if she was ever in the vicinity, I'd listen to his latest yogi-trotting adventures and smile politely in an attempt to hide any signs of admiration.

Earlier in the year, his relationship with the yoga master broke down (with her breaking half of the belongings in his apartment). I was somewhat disappointed he'd quickly took up with a glamorous French cosmetics executive; not exactly as spiritual as the last, but I resigned myself to not caring. Back then, I was probably still brooding over the journalist, hoping that Jacob would come back, or plotting how I might get Viktor to admit he liked me, whereas I should have been focusing on romantic prospects that were actually realistic.

Now, months later, with the American journalist behind me and Jacob's latest disappointment fresh in my mind, I was susceptibly open to other encounters. Perhaps Alain would invite over some sexy French media types? The Countess and Pussycat were away on holiday and thus not around to remind me what those guys were typically like.

I'd done many double evenings before. That said, they sometimes got me into trouble, like that night I shuttled from

Annie's birthday to Tad's party. Alain's message made it seem like a casual affair, so I could pop by for a few glasses of rosé then bop down to meet Thomas and Antoine, couldn't I?

I left the office at a decent hour and went home to change and freshen up before heading back out again. Alain only lived a twenty-minute walk or so from my place; however, about three blocks into my journey I was already regretting wearing a new pair of sparkly sandals, with small stiletto heels, I'd just bought. I could barely walk, and the bloody cobblestones in Montmartre were not making my task any easier! This was proof of the danger of impulsive and impractical purchases during the summer sales.

Luckily, with it being August, the *Vélib* stations were full, so I hopped on a bike and whizzed down the hill to his street in the 10th arrondissement, pulling up to his doorstep around 7:00 pm.

"Perfect timing!" Alain said cheerfully, welcoming me with open arms. "So lovely to see you, darling!"

Sitting around the coffee table in the living room in his very Parisian and charming wooden-beamed apartment was a cute video producer, Michel, and a saucy photographer, Thierry, both of whom I'd previously met, as well as another girl I'd never seen before; all were old friends of Alain and already well into the rosé.

I shuffled over in my silly new shoes to give them each the *bise* and squeezed into a cozy corner of the sofa with my own glass of rosé—it would help me forget about the blisters forming on the sides of my feet.

Since it was such a small group we all chatted together in French; about our new projects, summer plans, and why they weren't on holiday right now, like the vast majority of Parisians. Glasses were constantly refilled and voices, laughter, and stories rose with the increasing quantity of the rosé consumed.

THOMAS [08/03/2011 8:15 PM]
I think we'll actually be meeting up
at 9:30 PM instead. Antoine's
plane was delayed.

In that case, a refill of rosé wouldn't hurt; I had at least another half an hour to spare, plus I didn't have to show up exactly on time. Before long, another bottle of rosé was being opened and a joint was being passed around, both making the evening all the more rosier. I never did smoke very much... only when in Rome, or rather Amsterdam... or the spiritual loft of Alain.

"*Alors c'est fini avec la folle?*" I happened to catch Thierry asking Alain, while I was chatting to Michel. *La folle?* It's over with the crazy one? Were they talking about his girlfriend? I didn't know that things were on the rocks, nor that she was crazy, but considering his last girlfriend, it didn't seem out of the question for him to like 'fiery' women.

THOMAS [08/03/2011 10:12 PM]
As soon as you're free, we're
waiting for you on rue Soufflot!

Oh man, I was having such a good time, I'd almost forgotten about my original plans for the night. Could I really bear putting on those nasty shoes and shuffling across town to one of the least reachable subway stations? I'd have to change twice to get there with long subway corridors to painfully scuffle down, all just to meet up with overly eager Thomas and oddball Antoine.

I sent them a 'sorry can't make it' reply; I just didn't feel like going. Chilling out with these guys just seemed like the best way to end the week. Not to mention the fact I was getting really, really chilled out, and it was't thanks to the cool rosé.

> THOMAS 3/08/2011 10:59 PM
> Ok, but if you want to meet up at your place after midnight for an intellectual... and sensuellllle visit... or else on Sunday? Kisses

Oh la la! That was definitely a reply crafted by Antoine, there was no way that Thomas was capable of such efforts at seduction. I couldn't help but think back to that sunny afternoon when Antoine was the ringleader in our sensual afternoon in the park; who knows how far he might have tried taking things back at my place! Three of them! Triple *oh la la!* Meeting up with then after midnight sounded like a dangerous thing to do.

Another bottle of wine went around accompanied by another joint, but around 1:00 am Michel had itchy feet to go out dancing.

"*Allez...* Come on guys, Le T-Rex is just up the street," Michel was trying his darndest to get us to go with him;

perhaps he shouldn't have rolled up that last joint, which had made us all more dopey than keen to hit the dance floor.

He eventually won over Thierry, Alain and I; their gal friend decided to head home. We downed the rest of our drinks and slid our shoes on, me with a wince. As we were ambling up the street towards the club, Alain put his arm in mine, where it stayed as we waited in line.

"You come here so often, Michel, don't you have some way to bypass this *putain* of a line?" complained Thierry. Why was it so busy in August? Were other clubs closed for the holidays? Michel might still have been raring to go, however, our buzz was starting to wear off and the line was going nowhere.

"I have some champagne in the fridge! Why don't we just go back to my place?" offered up Thierry. All of them seemed to live within a few blocks of each other. It was just like in their childhood, romping around the suburban neighborhood they'd all grown up in, the only thing that had changed were the 'games' they played.

I thought I was *game* for whatever, and I was quite comfy lingering on Alain's arm. Was he exhibiting a-little-more-than-friendly affection for me? If things were 'over' with the girlfriend; he was available, right?

Michel wasn't budging, though didn't appear to care we were abandoning him. So, off our little threesome went, meandering the few short blocks to Thierry's place.

"*Santé!*"

The bottle of champagne was blissfully popped and Alain was rolling another joint as we settled in at Thierry's hip photographer's loft. The destiny had reversed on what I'd thought would be a calm August Friday night... and the night was far from over.

At some point, Alain began to tell us about some of his adventurous with his Balinese guru.

"In fact, it's not just a regular Balinese Hindu practice," Alain went on. "It's a cult of love."

A cult of love?

Like what kind of love? I was guessing not merely platonic!

"We were thinking of starting up a branch here in Paris," added Thierry seductively. "We could call it *ThierAlainology* and we would be the masters of its love circle."

Better a religion of love than of power and greed like those Scientologists! I started to chuckle, however, turning to Thierry, he seemed dead serious as he reached over and gently tucked a loose lock of my hair around my ear.

"Its main doctrines revolve around *le plaisir*." Pleasure, huh? Like a pleasant love of drinking champagne?

"We've been honing the rituals."

"And feel they've almost reached perfection, but we still need to do a little more testing." With the most sensual smile, Alain lent over and started kissing me on one side... then Thierry on the other. Before I could tell them that I was pretty much a Buddhist, they attempted to convert me into their cult.

Mon Dieu! Correction: *Mes Dieux!* No Gods or Goddesses heard my smothered call. The rosé-weed-champagne combo had a similar, though not quite as lethal effect as with Fervex thrown in. However, my good senses had been crushed into utter mush, ready to be indoctrinated into this cult of love, or rather, my worship of Alain. Thierry was charming, but not nearly as attractive as his best friend. If I were to go along with their plan, alluring Alain was indeed the bait. Soon, I was whisked to the heavens of the second floor and passionately worshipped for the next few hours.

Alain was just as godly as I could have imagined. Perhaps he was the incarnation of Ragaraja, a Buddhist deity who transforms worldly lust into spiritual enlightenment? Or was he Min, the Egyptian god of love, sexuality, reproduction, and sexual pleasure? Call him Eros or Kamadeva, Alain would definitely be incorporating the principles of the Kamasutra into his cult's philosophies.

Time had blurred with body lines. At some point, hours later, when our highs had been reduced to fatigue, Alain helped me find a taxi. We wished each other a nice rest of the lazy month of August. He was going away the following week, so there was no hope in wrangling a little one-on-one religious lesson with him. After one mystical night, my August would likely return to boredom.

I probably shouldn't have let myself be seduced into their 'rituals,' if I'd really had any hopes for something 'real' to happen with Alain. I'd only stayed because I was actually fond of him; otherwise I could have fended them off like I had with Antoine and his trio as well as those Argentinians in Madrid. Part of the problem with him was that he was very handsome and knew it. Slightly vain, self centered and passive-aggressive, I didn't think our personalities really matched, even if he seemed to be the perfect 'match.' The good looks were just an added bonus; I was more attracted to his charm, intelligence and originality. We were close in age, had common interests, and shared a love of storytelling, traveling, adventure and passion for life (albeit expressed in somewhat different ways!). Plus, unlike Jacob, Alain lived in Paris, his home base amidst his gallivanting. What exactly did he get up to during his trips? Even though he'd officially been with his yoga girlfriend for a number of years and rebounded directly to *La Folle*, I could see through this *seemingly* serial monogamy. With whom did he practice his cult of love? From what I gathered, his time in Bali was not spent solely meditating with his guru. I wouldn't want to know how many 'disciples' he'd attempted to convert around the world.

All things considered, I still harbored a small desire for him, but only if he were to have just *one* love goddess: me. The whole incident did provide a surprising twist to my romantic aspirations. That said, I was not expecting a divine intervention anytime in the immediate future. If he made some moves in the autumn, when he got back from holiday, I would take things from there. Although I was somewhat doubtful.

"You did what?!" exclaimed The Countess, almost spitting out her wine.

"So was he as good as he looks?" asked Pussycat rather naughtily.

I'd considered whether or not to tell the girls about my 'religious' experience with Alain (and Thierry), but then I let it slip out when we were discussing the hot wine god we'd met that very afternoon.

What I'd thought would be a dull rest of August took a happy turn when—after years of pestering—The Countess finally invited us down to her family's country house, a last minute invitation since her parents had decided to come later than planned. For a week, we'd reign over the beautiful lesser-known wine kingdom of Minervois. A short drive from the medieval city of Carcassonne, it was also a stone's throw from many, many reasonably priced vineyards. We spent most of our days stopping in at The Countess' favorite *vignerons* and at quaint little villages in between... that is, when I wasn't hanging out the window of the third floor trying to capture a 3G signal so I could download my work messages. After all, I was meant to be working three days of that week. This was proving to be more difficult than I'd imagined, although we'd found a nice wine bar by the Canal du Midi that had Wi-Fi, a saving grace in more ways than one.

"Sounds exciting!" chimed in Rose, a British friend who was gradually filling in Naughty's missing shoes. She was definitely more 'adventurous' than The Countess, who erred on the traditional side.

"What did I tell you about journalists?" scolded The Countess.

"Well, he's not really a journalist..." I slid in as I poured more wine into her glass. It was getting dark on the terrace, so perhaps I could distract them from my *oh la la* revelation by suggesting we go inside to cook dinner.

"Actually, he's worse! On printed paper you can't see the diminishing hair and increasing belly-size of *some* journalists; a TV reporter needs to maintain physical appearances and is thus naturally more narcissistic than his print counterparts," she precised, trying to press her point like a winemaker tries to squeeze out all the precious juice from his grapes.

"I might be willing to try out his love cult," said Rose saucily, having migrated to the edge of the courtyard so she could get a signal on her phone to Google him.

"What about that winemaker we met today, he was kind of cute?" she put forth, sending the evil eye to Rose for having propagated my actions.

"The one with missing teeth and dirty coveralls? How many glasses of wine had you had before that visit?" questioned Pussycat with a raised eyebrow. We'd spent the week joking that it would be perfect to meet a charming young, *single* winemaker and live happily ever after in oenological bliss. However, like my dreams of having a villa, I wasn't sure if I was ready to move to the countryside just yet.

"Okay, maybe that one wasn't the most attractive, but his wine was excellent," The Countess said in defense of her feeble matchmaking efforts. "I'm saving the cutest one for your birthday, Lily."

I was certainly content with spending the next day with my good friends accompanied by the succulent food and wine of the region; and cute boys could be the cherries on my birthday cake.

Even before we left the house for our outing the next day, which would include a stop in at this supposedly *beau vigneron*'s winery, I caught sight of my first cute boy of the day—on my phone.

> From: Viktor   Wednesday, August 17 2011 12:05 AM
> Subject: Happy Birthday! Look over your shoulder before opening ;-)
>
> Dear Lily,
>
> Happy Birthday! Looking forward to seeing you in person soon, here is something so you'll be sure to recognize me, though I hadn't changed too much.
>
> Viktor

Sacré Bleu! Or rather *sacré* birthday! In good form, Viktor hadn't forgotten about my birthday and he also hadn't let his athletic physique slip. There he was, again turned with his back to the camera, but this time he was looking over his shoulder—like he'd advised me to do in the subject of his message for completely different reasons—and he was much closer to the camera than in his other photos. Who needed sexy winemakers when they had godlike nature-lovers? Happy birthday to me!

"Watcha looking at?"

I whipped around to find Rose peering over my shoulder. I hadn't thought to follow Viktor's warning, as I was usually home alone when I'd received his emails!

"Wowsers! Whoooo's that?" she enquired, stepping on her tippy-toes trying to get a closer look.

"Ohhh… I want to see too!" said The Countess, who'd just come out onto the terrace with a beautifully arranged breakfast tray.

"What am I missing out on?" shouted Pussycat as she poked her head outside, coffee mug in hand. Caught off guard, Rose snatched my phone and was now zooming in on the photo.

"Not bad at all!" she said approvingly.

"Give that back!" I hissed, reaching for her hand, though she'd already passed the phone over to The Countess whose eyes widening from the sight of the screen.

"Oh my! Now I see why you're so interested in this 'Viktor' character," she smiled broadly.

"I was going to buy you a sexy firemen's calendar for your birthday, the kind they sell at the balls, but good thing I didn't. You definitely don't need it if you've got one of these images appearing in your inbox monthly," said practical Pussycat. A sly look came over her face and, though Rose and The Countess were blocking me, it appeared that she was clicking on the buttons on my phone screen.

"Hey! What are you doing? Give that back!" I crie, desperately struggling to get past the girls to pry it from her grip, but now it was three against one.

"I was just going to thank him... on *our* behalf!" she claimed innocently.

"How about this, we design an appropriate 'thank you' reply together later today?" I suggested as a last resort. It would be totally embarrassing if she'd click send; my hopes of finally advancing things to another level with Viktor would go up in smoke like the forest campfire in the background of his photo. The three girls conferred with glances exchanged back and forth and, after a painfully long minute, Pussycat relinquished the phone. I'd better put my thinking cap on... and make sure my passcode was activated on my phone.

Over the course of our lovely day wine tasting, we actually drove a little further to visit the vineyard of some of our friends from the wine fair (*not* Maurice!). On the way back, we stopped in at the place with the sexy *vigneron*, but sadly we were greeted by his less desirable father, who informed us that his son was out in the vines that day.

"Sooooo? What about that reply?" asked Rose on the ride back to our village. The sun was now creeping towards the horizon, casting a gorgeous golden glow over the vineyards.

"Oh, I haven't forgotten. In fact, Countess, why don't you pull over into that little lane up ahead." I'd been struck by the perfect inspiration.

Acquiring the assistance of Pussycat the photographer, we marched over to the edge of one of the lanes of grapes. They were the perfect height. I lowered my bra straps on either shoulder and hid them just low enough that it looked like I didn't have anything on. Pussycat aimed carefully and directed me into the best position to be hidden well enough by the leaves, with The Countess and Rose giggling in the background. *Voilà!* It was the perfect combination of my love for wine and Viktor's love of nature.

Send.

However, it wasn't Viktor who I heard from next.

> From: Jacob   Thursday, 18 August 2011 01:11 PM
> Subject: Bruxelles!
>
> Lily!
> Hey there, girlie - how are you? I hope your summer is going well! I've heard it's been hot in Paris.
>
> I'm so bummed we didn't get to connect while I was there... Now, we are enjoying a full-on holiday in Brussels! We have a really cool flat here, with a kitchen, yard, laundry, everything. So nice to have true time off in a European city, a real treat for us. This is way last minute and probably far out of the realm of possibility for you, but hey - wanna come to Brussels this weekend? ;)
>
> I've had travels and things planned most weekends here, but this is my last week and it's wide open. I have my own floor in the flat, totally cozy and cool. Just wanted to throw it out there in case you happened to have a free weekend as well. I'm here until Thursday of next week.
> Really hope you're enjoying the summer!
>
> Write back when u can :) xxx J

Jacob! What a sweetie! Perhaps my summer wouldn't end in romantic doldrums after all. As excited as I was about getting his message, we were very far from Paris and only due to return Sunday night... so while hopping up for the weekend sounded like an amazing idea, it wasn't going to happen for this one.

But why did it have to only be on the weekend? Brussels was a mere hour-and-twenty-minute train journey from Paris; it was practically like crossing from one end of the city to the other. So, I wrote him back, suggesting to go up the following Wednesday after work; it would be a bit of a long day (and night), but far from impossible. Unfortunately, this didn't work for Jacob as his band would be heading off to Spain very early the following morning.

Still down in the south and in holiday mode, the next time we were having a drink and Wi-Fi break at the bar along the Canal, I snapped up a ticket for the following Monday, the day after our return. It wasn't the most exciting night of the week, but that didn't matter... I was going up to spend time with Jacob, not have a wild Belgian night on the town.

But, once again, I underestimated just what a night out with Jacob could entail!

I might normally have been exhausted from arriving back into Paris around midnight; Pussycat, The Countess and I all on the same train (with her Highness traveling in first class), and transporting sixty-six bottles of wine. These were carefully packed in either the extra suitcase we'd brought, or in boxes placed on the trusted folding trolley I'd brought down. All my muscle aches vanished the next morning knowing the fun prospects of my evening.

The work day whizzed by, and at 4:00 pm I ducked out of work a smidgen early to hop on the subway to Gare du Nord. A feeling of glee spread over me as I settled into my seat on the high-speed Thalys train bound for the Belgian capital.

We only live once, I repeated to myself.

I hesitated over popping into the train bar carriage for a drink to put me in a festive mood, but my bliss was maintained by the fields of the Pas de Calais swaying and shimmering on the other side of the window in the late summer sun.

Since Jacob didn't have a cell phone, and he'd given me a very specific meeting point at a certain subway station, I'd given him a very precise time of 6:15 pm to come and meet me. I'd surely make it there by then.

I found my way easily to what I thought was the appointed place. I checked my phone and saw it was 6:16 pm, but there was no cute boy standing with open arms in sight. I had to learn patience; he'd likely show up any minute now. Five, ten minutes went by, but still no sexy, sunkissed musician.

Was I in the right place? I was starting to get a little antsy, as the scene seemed all too reminiscent of July when we hopelessly couldn't manage to connect at the Bastille Day party. What would I do if I couldn't find him? Find the nearest pub and drown my sorrows in Belgian beer? Take the train directly back to Paris? I calmed myself down and resumed my pacing back and forth on the exit platform.

"*Heeeyyyy* there, pretty lady!" greeted a voice from my left, accompanied by a more than passionate kiss, which sent us stumbling backwards. "Sooooo good to see you! Let's go, it's this way!"

Hand in hand, I assumed I was being whisked off to the house he was staying at, where I'd drop off my little overnight bag. Then we'd uncork the bottle of wine I'd brought him from my trip to the South, and then we'd go out for some dinner and drinks. However, it seemed like he had other plans…

Why had we met up all the way at this obscure stop if we were taking the subway again? Oh well, I was just glad we found each other. We jumped on the subway, me using the ticket I had from getting there from the train station.

"I don't bother getting tickets, I can talk my way around the checkers here, piece of cake," he said, ever the rebel just like back in Paris with the hotel night watchmen and the police. It was as he was speaking more that I realized Jacob was actually a little tipsy, more than one would expect for 6:30 pm.

He slid into an empty seat beside a middle aged Muslim couple. Jacob pulled me down on his lap and began making out with me, like he hadn't kissed anyone all century, his wandering hand drifting up my thigh, much to the muffled horror of the traditional couple next to us. Jacob didn't seem to care in the slightest, but I, being sober, was a little embarrassed. We only had a couple of stations to go and when we got off he busted into giggles and kisses. Some things never change, I thought. We exited the station into a sea of Flemish-style brick buildings, behind which a tall steeple emerged: the famous town hall.

"Oh man, which way is it…?" he drunkenly pondered.

"Which way is it to where?" I cautiously enquired.

"I think it's back this way… I'll just ask these *policiers*."

Uh oh. Policemen. Jacob doesn't have such a good track record with them…

"I can turn the data on on my phone…" I attempted, but it was too late, he was swerving towards the two Belgian cops he'd noticed standing nearby.

"Heyyy *Bonsoir!*" He accosted them. *Oh god, please don't get yourself arrested for disorderly conduct.* "*Où est le Sofitel?*" The Sofitel? Why were we going there? Of course the police didn't understand his accent, but after a little back and forth, Jacob had managed to understand their indications, and keep it together enough for them not to question his level of intoxication. Then, we wandered off in the general direction they'd pointed.

"So this producer from Canal Plus came up from Paris to see us." Ah, that explained the Sofitel part; the French liked to stay in their national hotel chains when abroad. "He's a blast! We've been drinking since noon!" And this explained the drunkenness. Damn, I guess I should have had that drink on the train after all.

Jacob went on to tell me the producer had come up to discuss a side project he and fellow band member Toni were working on. Was getting plastered midday normal for meetings in the music business? I doubted this was a regular meeting, nor a regular producer.

We tumbled into the elegant lounge of the Sofitel, to the sounds of raucous laughter coming from the bar. Not surprisingly, the source was Toni, their European band manager Romain, and two very young party-looking people.

"How about another Gin and Tonic?" they greeted, ordering up another round of drinks.

I clearly needed to catch up if I was going to think any of their jokes were moderately funny. I downed the half-finished drink Jacob had abandoned to come and pick me up, followed immediately by a few chugs of my new drink, apparently courtesy of Canal Plus. Young and ambitious, León couldn't have been more than twenty-five, and was already a high-flying TV and music producer. He was a cute French Jew, his charming geeky look accentuated by his short curly brown hair and retro-style glasses (alluring but not nearly as dreamy as 'Adrien Brody'!). Besides freely flashing his Canal Plus company credit card, his attitude showed that he came from money. The girl he was with turned out to be his sister, a pretty, laid-back art student whom Toni was eyeing up. The volume of our conversation went up a new notch with a yet another new round of cocktails. León, happy to have a break from speaking English with the boys all afternoon, started chatting with me.

"I hope you're not jealous of me talking to your girlfriend," he said, patting Jacob on the shoulder and interrupting his discussion with the others.

"She's not my girlfriend, *mon frère*," Jacob replied. Sure, I wasn't his 'girlfriend,' but I certainly wasn't just a friend and I certainly hadn't come up to Brussels to meet any boys other than Jacob! I probably would have been more annoyed with his statement had it not been for the two G&Ts now under my belt. However, I was still way behind in their day of drinking debauchery.

Content with Jacob's answer, León carried on chatting with me in French and ordered up another round of drinks. The bartender hesitated, then proceeded to make them; it was clear we were becoming unwanted, our Saturday night dive bar behavior clashing with the mild-mannered businessmen occupying the few other tables, on this work-week evening. It was more hunger than the dirty looks from the other bar patrons, which implored us to abandon the posh hotel bar at around 8:30 pm.

"I know this great little bistro not far from here… we can go there for a bite," suggested Jacob. So we sauntered in the direction of the large plaza next to the hotel that would lead us towards this restaurant. Approaching its wide set of steps, León suddenly picked me up, like a fireman would attempting to save someone from a burning building, and ran down the steps into the pedestrian square.

"What are you dooooooing?!" I screeched, my laughter and squirming throwing him off course (or was it the gin?) and we went tumbling to the ground in a fit of giggles. I felt like I was Europa being carted off by Zeus, just like in the paintings I'd studied back at art school. Like Zeus, it was clear that

León was used to getting what he wanted, one way or another. Real life wasn't as easy as mythology; he couldn't make me his by simple carrying me off. Besides, where was my hero to the rescue anyway?

Jacob's restaurant was not far, however, as we were about to go inside, the doorman put up his hand.

"*On va fermer,*" he informed us.

"Closing? No way, *monsieur,*" Jacob rebutted. "It's like, not even late."

What started as a friendly attempt at convincing them to serve us rapidly turned ugly; the strong-willed Jacob I'd seen with the night porter that night in Paris was coming back out. Their argument was seriously heating up. Was Belgian cuisine worth fighting over? Luckily, the band manager Romain still had enough common sense—or experience with these Jacob outbreaks—to calm him down enough and eventually pull him down the street.

"Never mind, we can go for *frites*—what's more Belgian than that!" declared León, and off we trotted to one of the city's popular outdoor 'French' fry eateries. The route to our new destination went through the city's beautiful Grand Place. I slowly looked around, taking in its lovely buildings, vibrant outdoor cafés and twinkling lights. This would be the most 'sightseeing' I'd be doing on this trip to Brussels.

Jacob's mood mellowed out with his *frites*. A serving of fries might not have been enough to soak up all the alcohol the group had consumed over the course of the day, but it would help... or so I thought.

We mopped up the last of the mayonnaise from the corners of the little plastic containers using our final fries, and then ambled towards the tourist center, where the boys had previously discovered some bars in that area, which would be open on a Monday night. Much like the Latin Quarter in Paris, we'd entered a maze of pedestrian, cobblestone streets bordering La Grande Place, trafficked only by travelers wooed into the bright, kitschy by their offerings of *moules-frites* and large pints of Belgian beer.

"It's this way!" said Jacob, guiding us down an even narrower laneway. For the time being, I'd managed to evade 'Zeus' and was walking arm-in-arm with Jacob listening to some of his latest touring adventures—a peaceful conversation abruptly interrupted by loud shouting from behind us.

We whipped around to see the rest of our group about ten feet back, in front of one of those touristy restaurants. León, who was holding his bleeding nose, encircled by a group of screaming waiters and Romain and Toni hollering back at them.

Amidst the chaos and shouting back and forth in French, I gathered that León had tripped and his head fell right into this massive, decorative beer glass on display outside the restaurant. But not just any restaurant... a Moroccan restaurant. Crap. León's Jewish heritage was more than obvious. The restaurant staff was demanding that he pay the extortionate amount of eighty-five Euros for the broken glass. There was no way it was worth that much, hence the ensuing verbal battle. Then León claimed they'd broken his glasses in the fall and possibly his nose. Things were once again heating up and it wasn't piping hot fries. Who then walks up to add some hot sauce to these *frites*? A new pair of *policiers*. This would either be a big *merde* or a big *merci*.

León's tone softened and suddenly he was offering to pay a smaller sum for the glass, a transaction that the police would hear none of. From what they could 'see,' this poor French tourist had merely fallen. what a bad impression of this pacifistic country, in the very capital city of Europe, if he were to be forced to pay for a simple accident. They sent us on our way, much to the restaurant staff's consternation.

As soon as we'd rounded the corner, León broke out into gut-busting laughter. It hadn't been an accident at all; he'd purposely head-butted the glass. Was it because he'd noticed it was an Arab restaurant or because he was just stupidly drunk? I tried to assume the latter of this additional strange twist to our evening... which I hoped would involve no more cops, or dumb and dangerous antics.

We'd arrived at our next stop, a famous Absinthe bar. *Hmmm*, after all their drinking maybe it wasn't such a good idea to move on to this strongest of alcohols, a favorite of 19th-Century artists, intellectuals and probably musicians, too. Then again, it did fit in perfectly with our crazy night. We selected a few glasses from their biblical menu and soon I had León hanging on me, his compliments increasing with his heightened tipsiness, and Jacob... well, I wasn't sure where he was.

"Let's go check out the bar across the street," Jacob whispered in my ear, magically appearing just as Léon was passing the over-flirtatious mark. With that, we snuck away on our own and escaped Zeus' advances.

I shouldn't have been surprised that in their few weeks in town, Jacob and Toni had discovered *all* the hotspots in town. Down we crawled into the depths of a bizarre cellar to discover a cavernous underground bar. Jacob got us some drinks, while I befriended a quirky couple from a small nearby Flemish village.

"*Santé!*" we cheered, our beer steins echoing our toast.

Soon we'd also befriended two mid-forties gents from Bristol in town for business, who tried to flirt with me while Jacob went to get us another drink. This time Jacob didn't pull the 'she's not my girlfriend' card, but instead escorted me back to the cool house they'd been put up in. Not like I saw much of the house—besides Jacob's room.

With only an hour or so of sleep, I miraculously heard my alarm at 5:45 am, beckoning me to my 7:00 am train. I was miserable to leave. As much as the night hadn't been what I'd expected, it was the usual Jacob magic: surprises, stories, and living in the moment. I splashed some water on my face, tied my crazy hair back in a bun, and put back on my not too skanky, beer splashed clothes from the previous night. Jacob looked so calm and cute in his sleep, and all I wanted to do was crawl back into bed beside him. Instead, I gave him a delicate peck on the cheek and crept out of the house, the soft morning light leading my way along the train tracks to the closest subway station, the one I'd met Jacob at twelve hours previously. I wasn't sure when our paths would cross again, yet I was certain they would.

Fortunately, I had time to grab a double cappuccino and croissant before boarding the train. As soon as we pushed off south, I was regretting my decision. Why couldn't I be like Jacob and live in the moment—*completely*? Why didn't I just call in sick and go back to Paris the next day? I never took sick days and these were unlimited at my company! I'd even worked every day back in July, when I was actually very sick with bronchitis, a senseless act, which led me to overdosing on Fervex and mucking up my opportunity to see Jacob. My serious work ethic always won out... or almost...

From: Sofia   Monday, August 22 2011 9:45 PM

Ciao Lily!

Jimmy is playing this weekend down in Spain for this festival. Come, come, come!!

Un bacio, Sofia

Sofia's message had actually come in while I was roaming the streets of Brussels, with that riotous brat pack. I did recall that Jacob had mentioned he was playing in a festival in Spain the following weekend, but I hadn't given any consideration whatsoever to going down. It had to be the same as the one Sofia was trying to get me to go to. I hadn't expected I would see Jacob that soon. Could I really manage to get away again after my recent working holiday and then the last minute trip to Brussels? My arm was oh so easily twisted for a fun cause.

The festival took place in two extremes of the country: Benidorm in the southeast, and Santander in the northwest. As it stood, Sofia was already going to be down in Valencia for work, so she was planning on renting a car from there and driving the hour and a half to attend the first night of the festival taking place Friday night... then she would careen through the country on Saturday to reach Santander, for the second night of the festival. Was this slightly insane?

Well, I'd just gone to Brussels for the night, so this would just be one step up.

I spent Tuesday night looking at all the flight options possible. Alas, there seemed to be absolutely no way of getting from Paris to Benidorm on Friday afternoon in time for the concert. Even trying to make it just for the concert in Santander on Saturday seemed next to impossible, as there were no direct flights from Paris and I would have to fly to Biarritz (in the extreme southwest of France), and then cross the border from there by bus, or else take an expensive flight to San Sebastian, Spain. From there, I would still have to take the bus to reach Santander. The most viable solution was to go down to meet Sofia on Thursday night. This would mean skipping out on work on the Friday. Could I do it?

From: Jacob   Wednesday, August 24 2011 3:16 PM
Subject: Espana!

Hey Lil,
No way, that is glorious news! I admire your gusto :)

As our band manager Romain is not going to be with us, I really don't know yet how easy everything will be, but I'm pretty certain that getting you a pass should be ok. Are you guys driving to the two shows? I think they're quite far from each other, and I'm pretty sure that we'll be too tight in the van to take on more passengers. Anyways, it will be exciting! And so good to see you again.

I don't have the number of Santi, our Spanish tour manager, but hopefully I will be able to get it to you once we arrive in Madrid tomorrow.

Yayyy! Travel safe, and I'll see you in España!
XO J

Yes, I could. We only live once and, *cough, cough*... that bronchitis seemed to be coming back.

A feeling of nervous excitement ran through me as I jumped on the suburban train to Orly Airport after work on Thursday, clutching my passport and a very small carry-on bag. Sofia had taken care of most of the arrangements; she'd booked us a twin room at a hotel in Valencia for that night and the rental car would be ready to pick up the following day. I was to take a taxi there from the airport.

Spain really lives for the night, and my arrival around 9:00 pm was just in time for dinner. Sofia and I caught up on a lively terrace over some tapas and *vino tinto*.

"*Salud!*" we cheers-ed enthusiastically to the beginning of our audacious, rock'n'roll weekend.

"Since I have to work in the morning, you can visit the sites in town. I'll text you when I'm done, then we'll get the car and off we go!" said Sofia, explaining the game plan for the next day.

I didn't really know what I was in for, but I was ready for some adventure. Now, all I had to do was call in sick—for the first time in my life.

At least I didn't have to actually 'call' anyone, I just had to send around an email to my colleagues letting them know I was ill. Considering most of them used our unlimited sick day policy from time to time, I really shouldn't have felt guilty, or so I tried to convince myself.

Early the following morning, I pulled out my phone and spent way too long crafting a convincing yet brief email outlining my purported *maladie* confining me to a bed. I left out which country that bed was in. I clicked send and breathed a sigh of relief. Even before I finished my respiration, my phone buzzed with a text message. *Ah!* Had I been caught already?

My heartbeat quickened as I slowly turned over my phone to see what it was. No, I wasn't being checked up on. It was just one of the guides back in Paris trying to get out of a tour for that morning. He was magnificent in all other ways, but he never followed protocol and resorted to simply texting me, whenever he needed anything. I was not going to attempt to help him, so I texted him a reminder to call our emergency line (i.e. leave me alone to enjoy my fake sick day) and took a second deep breath. Thankfully, I wasn't bothered again and the rest of my 'sick day' passed without any other work-related issues, except for a deluge of sweet 'get better soon' messages from my colleagues. That throat was already starting to feel better thanks to a warm *café con leche*.

I'd been to many parts of Spain, during that infamous backpacking trip and on a few subsequent journeys to the Iberian peninsula, but I'd never been to Valencia, the country's third largest city. So I had a nice time wandering the winding streets and picturesque plazas of the historic core, taking pictures of imposing medieval towers, the eclectic cathedral and cool vintage signs. However, I couldn't even post these photos on Facebook, they would blow my fake illness cover right out of the Mediterranean waters. After a few hours, Sofia sent me a message with a designated meeting point, where we grabbed a quick bite and officially began our road trip.

The stretch of Spanish coastline south of Valencia around Alicante had been drastically altered in the first decade of the 21st Century, when much of the once picturesque Costa Blanca was overtaken by horrendous, massive holiday resorts populated by hordes of thrifty sunseekers. The construction of some of these behemoth buildings came to a grinding halt when the Spanish property bubble burst in 2008.

I'd heard tales of the coast's gaudiness, although, nothing could prepare me for the dreadful sight of the tacky towers on the outskirts of our destination: Benidorm. Clouds had even crept over the previously sunny sky, or perhaps they permanently hung over this dismal city?

We certainly weren't tempted to explore the town, even if we had arrived a little early. We immediately went in search of the concert venue, hoping it might already be open, or hoping to go somewhere else nearby, where we could comfort our souls with the help of a crisp *cerveza* and have a break from the architectural nightmare we found ourselves in.

Arriving at the venue, it wasn't exactly what I'd expected for a 'festival,' which I normally associated with a vast outdoor area, mud, and thousands of people thrashing about. In fact, this summer Jacob had been playing at some of the biggest music festivals around Europe, including France's largest, Les Vieilles Charrues, which attracts 200,000 attendees. We seemed to be at a small old warehouse, which had been converted into a cultural center (at least there was some 'culture' in Benidorm). It didn't matter if there were 10 or 10,000 people, we would surely have a blast.

As we'd hoped, the venue was open and Jacob had added us to the list as promised. Once inside, we found the narrow hall virtually empty. True to Spanish tradition, even though the show began at 7:00 pm, few people were there for the first band, as they were probably still having their afternoon *siesta*. Sofia and I got our *cervezas* and kept a lookout for our band friends. The festival-goers gradually trickled in with the passing hours and probably numbered in the hundreds by the time the room got hopping around 9:00 pm.

"*Hola*, baby!" greeted Jacob with a kiss on the cheek, sliding his arm around my waist. *Ahhh*, he looked really sexy tonight. It was hard to believe it'd been less than a week since our crazy night in Brussels. Would tonight be just as insane?

Jimmy was playing around 11:00 pm and Jacob's band would be coming on sometime after midnight, so one thing was certain: it was going to be a late night. Now and then, the boys would swing by and hang out with us, but it wouldn't be until after they played that they'd really be free. No matter, Sofia and I were enjoying our beers and having a good time discovering each new band.

As could be expected, she lit up when Jimmy and his band hopped on stage. Their energy was just as electric as the first time I'd seen them back on that fateful November night. Jacob's band was also on fire, fueled by the high voltage response from the small but feisty audience.

Afterwards, Jacob had managed to convince the bouncer to let Sofia and I backstage. This turned out to merely be the courtyard garden behind the stage, which was now milling with band members, crew and their friends. Sofia was hanging out mostly with Jimmy, Bob and other members of their band, and I was sitting with Jacob and Toni, just drinking beers, listening to fun band stories to the backdrop of the remaining bands, still going strong back inside.

"Hey Lily, why don't we get a start on our drive," said Sofia, coming over to Jacob and I around 4:00 am.

"But Sofia, it's so late. Why don't we just stay here, get a few hours sleep, and take off early tomorrow... well... today?" I lobbied, not seeing the sense of starting our drive this late.

"Come on, Sofia," added in Jacob. "Don't be silly. You can head up after a few hours sleep. We're leaving in the morning, too."

"Silly? Don't call me silly," retorted Sofia. "Lily, if you want to stay, maybe you can get a ride in Jacob's band van then."

Back and forth we went, and the more we pleaded, the more Sofia wanted to leave. In addition to the late hour and fatigue, we'd all been sipping away at those *cervezas* for hours and hours. It wasn't exactly safe to be driving at night, on roads we didn't know.

"Fine, I'm leaving here at least!" And with that, she stormed off.

Mierda. That was not good. There was definitely not enough room in Jacob's band van... and absolutely no other way to get from Benidorm to Santander... Madrid... Paris... anywhere! Sofia also had my bag with my passport in the trunk of her car. Massive *mierda*. I'd figure a way out of this mess later. Worst case scenario, maybe another band could give me a ride. No use wallowing in despair, another *cerveza* and a passionate kiss from Jacob would help.

After a while, she did text something about seeing me in the morning and that she'd be getting a hotel nearby, so that was a bit of a relief. With the concert now finished, Jacob and I went back to his hotel. I set an early alarm... not like I'd really need it in my present seductive company. Benidorm wasn't exactly Brussels, but it still had presented some twists in our weekend plan.

Sofia did text me around 7:00 am to tell me where to meet her. The silence in the car was deafening. Outside, the heat was hovering off the barren dry landscape of the plains of central Spain. Inside the car it was cool, though it wasn't the A/C that was keeping the air icy.

While it made more sense *not* to drive at 4:00 am, Sofia had been entirely right. She knew her own driving abilities and if she'd wanted to leave, I shouldn't have disputed her desire. Sure, while I was thinking of safety first... there's no denying the fact I also wanted to spend more time with Jacob, and that simply wasn't fair to her. I'd really lost the friend award that night and was paying my dues in silence. I couldn't even sleep because I felt like I should be a good co-passenger and try to keep her awake with pleasant chatter. But it just wasn't going to happen, and we proceeded quietly on our musical mission across the country.

At some point, we stopped for gas and a sandwich, but otherwise it was full throttle ahead. We ran into some Saturday afternoon traffic around Madrid. Despite taking the highway bypassing the congested city, we were slowed to a crawl.

We'd been making good time, but this little hurdle was going make our arrival time very tight. Tonight's festival started in the late afternoon and Jimmy's band was on a 6:30 pm sharp. With the Madrid traffic madness behind us around 4:00 pm, Sofia finally started warming up; we were nearing our destination and were likely to arrive in a couple of hours.

"Crap, there's a fork coming up in the road; which way should we go?" Sofia sudden asked, thrusting the map at me. I scampered to find where we were. Indeed, it was showing there were two ways of getting to Santander. Based on the map, the one to the right looked marginally faster, so I pointed to the upcoming exit ramp.

This new highway started off fine, and Sofia's mood improved even more when we put on Jimmy's latest album. However, very quickly the road took an... unexpected turn. Or rather turns. We rounded a corner and found ourselves on a two-lane road clinging to a giant canyon. *Santos cielos!* This wasn't indicated on the map! But then again it wasn't the kind that showed depth. Even if it did, I was in no shape nor had enough time to realize what terrain the N-623 had in store for us...

It was 5:15 pm, and we'd made it safely around the canyon and Sofia was trying to pass a slow delivery truck ahead of us. We rounded another corner and came face to face with another obstacle: a huge valley with a lake in the middle! The only way around it seemed to be on this winding two-lane road hugging the sides of the valley! Boy was it beautiful, but hardly enjoyable at the speed Sofia was going. It was like a scene in an action movie, but there was no way Sofia was going to let this become 'mission impossible.'

Her brief journey into happiness had descended into a trip down the River Styx. We somehow made it safely to the end of this roadway nightmare and could see city limits of Santander around 6:10 pm. Luckily, the town had good signage guiding us to the concert venue, otherwise we would have been totally screwed.

Still, as we got closer, we did go around a couple of roundabouts twice, trying to figure out which exit was the right one. The sound of distant music eventually led us to our destination. Since it was a bright sunny day on the Galician coast, there was no parking around the park where the festival band shell was located. The spaces around it were filled by fellow concert-goers or locals enjoying a weekend stroll.

"Fuck it!" roared Sofia, jamming the rental into a tiny, possibly illegal space (*Please, please, parking angels, protect the car from being towed!*). We grabbed our bare concert necessities and ran towards the festival entrance. During our sprint we could hear Jimmy's band already on stage, but luckily we'd only missed two songs. Sofia had returned to her normal positive self, and the last thing I wanted was for this to be derailed by missing the band she'd driven all this way to see.

"I'm sorry about yesterday," she said, turning to me after a few songs.

"I'm really sorry too," I genuinely replied.

We gave each other a big hug, said a few more words of apology and then it was like nothing had ever happened. Though I did make an internal pledge to be more attentive to my friends' requests in the future. Now the fun could truly commence. After I had a much needed Red Bull.

This venue was a lot bigger than the previous night's. The large bandshell was set into a sunken slope of lawn for casual outdoor seating. At full capacity, it could probably fit 5,000, if not more. Tonight there were easily about a thousand festival attendees.

When Jimmy's set was over, Sofia caught sight of a band friend of hers and she went to say hello, while I went in search of Jacob. I found him on the mezzanine deck chatting with some musicians from another band. It turned out this other band had been pretty popular back in the '70s. Now, they were trying to make a comeback. At some point, Jacob had to go backstage to get ready for their set and I was left chatting with one of the members of this other band.

"You don't have a backstage pass?" he said. "Wait here, I'll get you one."

I don't know why Jacob hadn't done the same if they were so easy to acquire. Just like that, I was a special guest of this geezer rock group. Hanging out a little longer with my backstage-bestower, he came out with a "You know, you're pretty cute."

Yikes! Why does everything come at a price? I definitely didn't find him 'pretty cute.' He looked about Maurice's true age, without the use of an *aspiride*.

"Um thanks, but I'm kind of with Jacob..." Just kind of. On one hand, it might have been better for Jacob to have been around, yet on the other, he may have told him I wasn't his girlfriend, like he'd said to the young producer back in Brussels.

I made up some excuse that allowed me to escape his flirtations. With my backstage pass looped around my neck, I returned downstairs to find Sofia. After Jacob's band had played, I pestered him into acquiring a pass for Sofia as well. From then on, we cruised between the pit and the backstage lounges having beers and uproarious laughs with the musicians.

This was light years away from what could have been my Saturday night destiny of watching movies in the Parisian suburbs, had I settled for one of the other stable, yet sleepy, romantic candidates of the previous years. Yet, deep down inside, I knew I was like Cinderella at the ball; the magic was bound to come to an end. For this specific night, it happened at 4:00 am instead of midnight, when Jacob had to go back to his hotel, alone. He was exhausted and had to play another gig the following night. So, we bid each other a long tender goodbye, a farewell bringing to a close our great week-long adventure from Brussels to Galicia. These were the most unlikely places for the most unlikely romance.

VANCOUVER: THE FINAL FRONTIER?

MY FLEETING musical Prince Charming was heading off into the California sunset. He thought he might be coming back later in the fall, but nothing was for sure. The only concrete thing was that, while this had been a fun summer, I was 'not his girlfriend.' It was an impossible romance that was like a catchy love song, stuck on repeat. Even if he did come back in a few months' time, it would be the same old tune. It had been an exciting distraction, but now with autumn approaching, my trip to Canada was also coming up. I had to decide what to do about Viktor.

He'd promised me he'd in town all of October, so it looked like our reunion would finally and fatefully be taking place. I had absolutely no intention of leaving the city without seeing him, nor any intention of leaving without some clarity on his feelings for me. It was time to face the music; whether it would be to the tune of *L'Hymne à L'Amour* or *Les Histoires d'Amour Finissent Mal... en Général,* I had to dance to the rythme of *Je Ne Regrette Rien.*

No regrets.

I was trying to repress my anxiety. However, over the course of the week at my mom's place, it did nothing but surge. The fresh air enjoyed on strolls along the ocean promenade only provided me with temporary mental relief. How was I going to approach Viktor? What was it going to be like? Ten years ago, we were nothing but wistful university students. Diploma in hand, we'd set off to explore the world in completely opposite directions, me to Europe and he to Asia. Despite this, our paths intersected on so many occasions, without us being aware of it. Now, a decade later, was fate finally converging our courses?

It was only then that I started asking myself some real questions. Questions about the practicality of these lofty dreams I'd devised about potentially returning home for love. I thought I could give up all my European adventures for a new start back home, but would doing so for the right person be enough motivation? Naughty seemed happy with her fresh start, and didn't seem to be missing Paris too much, yet. Would it be the same for me? As always, I was jumping way ahead of myself.

From: Princess Jess   Thursday, October 132011 9:10 AM
Subject: Possible EMERGENCY!

Dearest Princess,

I'm really sorry to write with bad news, but our cottage is flooded and we need to go urgently to check out the damage. I'm not sure we'll be back on Sunday in time for your arrival, but I'll let you know asap. Is there anyone else you could stay with in Vancouver just in case?

SO SORRY!
Princess J

Damn, that wasn't good. Or was it? There was *one* person whom I thought could put me up. Viktor. It just might be the perfect setting for us to really talk. Perhaps this was a blessing in disguise? I tried not to get too excited and fatalistic while I carefully crafted him an email to see if I could stay at his place. I held my breath as I hit send, and then immediately fled outdoors for a calming walk by the sea.

My stroll allowed me to further contemplate the situation. It was really gorgeous out here on the West Coast. The landscape was exceptionally beautiful, the climate was mild, the people were super friendly. While my Mom's city was sleepy, Vancouver was a thriving, cosmopolitan metropolis, but only a short journey by ferry or plane away from her. I'd even developed some Vancouver-based contacts through work who'd occasionally slipped in that they'd love to work with me more closely, so I might even have a ready-made job. I was set on so many fronts... this one missing romantic piece just had to fall into place. And it very well could by the end of the week.

I stayed on this nervous high for the rest of the day, until I checked my emails after dinner, seeing my inbox flashing with a message from Viktor. I tried to contain my delight as I clicked into it.

From: Viktor   Thursday, October 13 2011 8:42 PM
Subject: Vancouver bound

Hi Lily,

I will book the day in my calendar, and you are welcome to stay that night. I have an inflatable mattress or a very comfy couch. The bed is comfy too, but my girlfriend just moved into that. Do you need me to pick you up from the airport? Any idea what you want to do?

With love,
Viktor

His girlfriend? What girlfriend? That just wasn't possible!

My emotions went from terror to disbelief to sorrow and back around like the crashing waves of the Pacific Ocean. Emerging from my state of shock, certain things actually started to make sense. A girlfriend would explain why he never made time to stop by Paris. Had he been traveling with said girlfriend on all those trips to Africa, Japan and Malaysia? While that might seem like a logical explanation, what about all of his 'I'm thinking of you,' 'with loves'... and all those racy photos?

Trying to grasp this very unexpected revelation, the words of the psychics floated to the surface of my confused mind. They'd both said that my soul mate would be in another relationship—or just getting out of one—when we met. This double prophesy is what had incited me to give the likes of cheating Mario and Jacques with his secret wives more of a chance than they'd deserved. Plus, it had given me that extra push to suggest dinner with married Count Hugues when I should have just told him to get on the next plane to Tahiti and stay there. However, each time that little devil in my mind convinced me to keep an open mind about these men because maybe, just maybe, they were *the* one the fortune-tellers predicted.

The 'girlfriend just moving in' part with Viktor was what didn't really jive with my supposed destined 'soul mate.' If they were moving in together, that most likely meant that they'd been together for a while (i.e. at least when he'd sent me the last few photos), and that things must be serious. Geez, how serious could they really be if he was sending naughty messages to someone else? I barely slept that night with these thoughts racing through my mind.

> From: Princess Jess   Friday, October 14 2011 8:04 AM
> Subject: Good news!
>
> So looks like the flood wasn't as bad as we'd thought. I'll be there to pick you up from the bus station. What time do you get in?
>
> xoxo Princess J

Phew! I was saved from the awkwardness of having to meet *and* sleep under the same roof as his 'girlfriend,' but I still didn't fully know what to make of the situation. Even if I did see Viktor, there would be no confronting him to try to uncover his real feelings for me, not if my pride had anything to do with it.

"What??" exclaimed Princess Jess on hearing the latest twist to the Viktor saga.

"I just don't know what to think," I lamented, popping a thick chunk of organic brie onto a seven grain cracker before taking a sip of my glass of Okanagan Valley natural wine. I was treated to a true princess welcome when we arrived back at Jess' place: a huge *apéro*, British Columbia-style.

"Do you want me to bring Bill along? He can take him into the back alley and kick his pretty, firm ass," she offered, pouring me a gigantic North American refill. I was still going to see Viktor, but was bringing Jess as a buffer.

"That wouldn't be very Canadian of us, would it?"

"He used to be a hockey player. He has experience," she elaborated, convincingly pimping out her husband's muscleman services.

"I guess it's better I found out before seeing him tonight and potentially making an enormous fool of myself." I was still left utterly flabbergasted... but not completely without hope. "Maybe there's something I don't know about his situation?"

"Like that he's a total cad?" *Uh oh.* She was getting worked up—maybe she'd be the one taking him into the back alley.

"Um well, perhaps in Namibia the word girlfriend means a 'girl' friend?"

"Oh, please. She's just never come across his camera roll. Now that they are living together, he'd better log out of his email every time or else he risks her coming across some unpleasant messages..."

Of course she was right; however, I didn't think I could finally be in the same city as him, after all of these years and all of these missed encounters, and not see him. The sparks could fly, cupid's arrow could strike, or at the very least I would see an 'old friend' after ten years. The bottle of wine Jess and I were polishing off would certainly help.

From: Viktor   Monday, October 17 2011 8:02 AM
Subject: Thanks for the visit

Hey Lily,

Thanks for the visit - was really great to see you again. You really are just as wonderful as I remember you, still haven't seen you with your clothes off though, so can't cross that one off the list ;-)

When are you going to post those pics?
Let me know when you are back through town again, as I would love to catch up again.

With love,
Viktor

We were ten minutes late. I could see what I knew must be his figure shivering in front of the Mexican restaurant, where we'd chosen to meet. It turned out that he and Jess lived a mere six blocks away from each other in this sprawling city. They'd probably unknowingly bumped carts at the supermarket, or been in line behind each other at some cold-brew hipster coffee place at some point.

As he'd described me in his email sent the next morning, he was also just as wonderful as I'd remembered him. The small curl of his lips when he smiled; the sparkle of his olive-green eyes; his to-die-for accent... my cheesy, sticky burrito was the only thing holding my heart together and my Margarita the only thing keeping me from bursting into tears right there in front of him.

Jess helped keep the conversation light and on a safe track, but when he went to the restrooms, she reminded me of her offer to take him out back to the alley. How fortunate I was to have these amazing friends spread across the globe. They are the ones who have always stood by me whether it was in Paris, Barcelona or Vancouver. The night ended without injury, really; only my heart had been put through the emotional wringer (on what seemed like an endless spin cycle).

I skimmed Viktor's message that morning when I saw it come in, but it wasn't until later on, after a tearful farewell to my Princess at the airport, that I really thought about it. It might have been nice for him to find me 'still wonderful,' but had this all been a game for him? He'd have to leave one thing crossed off that life list he had.

With great resolve, I ordered an over-priced glass of wine at the airport bar and drafted him a reply. It wasn't one worthy of the verbal butt-kicking that he deserved, but I had to address the question over why he'd been sending me those naughty photos when he had a girlfriend all along, or at the very least, the last couple of years.

From: Viktor   Wednesday, October 19 2011 9:45 AM
Subject: re: re: Thanks for the visit

Hey Lily,

About giving me a hard time - don't worry about it. I totally
deserve it! I don't really know how to explain it. I like being
friends with you, and perhaps sharing pictures with you is
an expression of a desire to misbehave, and a desire to
see such a beautiful lady with her clothes off!

Travelling around the world finding unusual places to take
pics for you is kind of a way for me to share more of a
connection with you, and the thought that you might also
get pleasure out of what I sent, also very motivating. I
guess I didn't really think about how it would make you
feel, or that acknowledging that it happened face to face is
a full admission of what an inspiration you have been to
some amazing solo photos?

Hmmm. I don't really know.
Well, let's catch up again soon, and I hope I haven't made
you feel awkward!

xo V

The response awaiting me as I touched down at Charles de
Gaulle Airport was not exactly what I'd been expecting. Had
he just been trying to get a rise out of me, or more of a
connection? What was the point of creating a 'connection'
with one girl if one were already in a relationship with
another? It doesn't seem very normal to send one's buddies
racy photos and to tell them they are thinking of them often.

Seeing him had been fabulous, painful and useful. In our
previous correspondence we'd rarely talked about interests,
habits and hobbies. Reacquainting ourselves over dinner did

make me wonder if we were even a good match to begin with, as we were very different in someways. He was a sporty-outdoorsy type, I was an artsy museum-goer. He went to bed early. I was a night owl. He'd ordered an orange juice at the restaurant, and I another Margarita.

I mean, opposites do attract sometimes, but that wasn't the issue. Since reconnecting I'd be gradually building up an image of the person I'd wanted him to be: an exciting, international man of mystery that destiny had returned to me; at the right time (what I thought was the fated 'later' predicted by the fortune-tellers). I decided, finally, I was no longer going to let supposed 'fate' dictate my romantic choices. For real this time. I could break those chains, and I could and would do it without Viktor. Determined conviction would help me move forward, to what exactly, I was not sure. All I knew at that very moment, was it would take a while to find a permanent cure for my heartache blues.

From: Jacob   Friday, October 22 2011 6:32 PM
Subject: Card received!

Hi Lily,

I got your postcard, thanks so much! And how exciting that you'll get to spend some more time in Spain.
Everything's cool here in LA, great to be home. I'm staying very busy and having a great time. We just found out that we'll be going to Brazil in December! Soooooo excited.
And yes, we will be coming back to France before the holidays. I'm not sure where just yet.
Glad to hear you're doing so well! Take it easy, stay warm, I'll send you some Cali sunshine!

Xoxo J

In the short term, I sought a temporary one. I'd sent him a postcard from Barcelona, where I'd gone for work before my trip home. The city where Jacob and I had met almost a year ago and from where all of our ensuing adventures had begun. The thought of seeing him in a month's time kept some of my depression at bay, once again a convenient bandaid patching up this new romantic void.

I must have replied not long after, perhaps a week or so, but the month of November passed slowly without any news from Jacob. Strange, I thought, he usually replied within a week or two. To the detriment of their privacy, public figures are easy to track down. Jacob had an open Facebook page to connect with fans and, way back when we'd met, he'd told me that he preferred to use email to stay in touch with close friends and family. As such, we weren't even Facebook friends, however, I knew I could find out where he was through this means of mass communication. Sure enough, they were currently in Brazil. Well, obviously he was too busy soaking up the sun and drinking caipirinhas to reply to me, which I could totally understand. However, as we crept into December, I figured he'd have to know his upcoming trip dates for France by now.

During another mild stalking session, I found his French tour schedule... which pegged them at that very moment in the South of France. Oh, Jacob! I was rather miffed he hadn't let me know he was on French soil. That wasn't like him. Besides that, my intuition told me he'd been drifting away over the past few months. Or was it really just his packed schedule?

It was entirely possible they weren't even going to be playing anywhere near Paris on this trip, since they'd already played here several times in the past year. However, upon closer examination of their schedule, I saw they had a show in a nearby suburb the following week. It was time for me to take action if I wanted to be sure to see him, so I sent him an email nudge.

> From: Jacob   Sunday, December 4 2011 10:18 AM
> Subject: re: Bienvenue en France
>
> Hi Lily!
>
> Yeah, we will be in Fontenay on Thursday - didn't know if it wasn't too far, would be great to see you too! And if you can bring Pussycat along, we'll have fun!
>
> Excited to hear your news, hope all is well. Lemme know and I'll make sure you have 2 on the list in Fontenay.
>
> Xoxo J

Though brief, his usual bubbly tone put any worries out of my head and I got psyched up for a fun night in... Fontenay? The family-oriented suburb in the west of Paris would hardly be considered lively, but as Jacob had proven in the past, fun can be had in the most unusual of places.

> PUSSYCAT [12/03/11 3:46 PM]
> I thought it was next Thursday,
> Sorry can't come!

Darn! Now that Pussycat was out, I needed to find a willing concert-goer. I couldn't invite The Countess, as this was totally not her style... What about Clém? This cute and cheerful French friend was a good partner in crime. She was single and keen on meeting someone new, a social concert might be good hunting terrain. I figured this might make her a little more likely to take me up on a not-so-tempting offer to hike out to the 'burbs.

CLEM 12/03/11 5:53 PM]
Why not? Sounds fun!

Excellent! I wasn't about to go out all by myself, so this way I could still attend. I dragged some concert-appropriate black clothes from my closet and met up with Clém at a junction of the suburban train: direction Fontenay-sous-Bois.

I wasn't expecting a cool club or anything; in fact, the concert was taking place in the local *salle de spectacle*, which turned out to be a not all that small community center for a suburban town. We got our comped tickets and Clém treated me to a beer as we waited for the concert to begin.

"Hey there, gurllll!" greeted Jacob, giving me *la bise* followed by a big hug. *Ahhhh!* It was always nice to see my ray of California sunshine. I introduced Jacob to Clém and we had a nice little catch-up chat before the opening act started. No, it wasn't a cool grungy rock band like at the previous concerts I'd attended with Jacob. This time it was a quirky old French rocker, a short, slicked-back-hair-type who was making a comeback (or trying too). Maybe the hall's booking agent had to please all audiences in one night out here in the suburbs? We had fun nonetheless. Jacob hung out with us for most of the set, and the drummer Toni popped around now and then when he wasn't off flirting with other girls.

A few songs before the end, Jacob gave me a kiss on the cheek and said, "See you girls after the concert."

Well, a kiss on just one cheek was certainly more affectionate than a simple *bise* farewell on both cheeks, I thought. Perhaps my intuition had been wrong?

Clém and I got another beer and positioned ourselves near the front of the stage in anticipation of Jacob's band to start. They played a great set and, in no time, had the fans of Fontenay rocking. After two lively encores, the curtains were definitively closed and we waiting around for the band to come out. They trickled out before too long, and Jacob was instantly at our sides again.

"I can't stay out too, too late tonight. We've been playing for six days straight and I'm totally wiped," said Jacob after a little while. I thought that just meant we just wouldn't stay hanging out with the *others* too late and we'd sneak off to his hotel alone. He was his super friendly self, and made Clém feel totally at home.

"I should probably get going," said Clém noticing that the clock was approaching midnight. Jacob and his friends seemed to be going strong and she was fine returning back to Paris on her own. After all, we weren't in a sketchy suburb, so she shouldn't have any troubles getting back into the city safe and sound by herself.

Soon Toni was off chatting with some Fontenay groupies and Jacob and I were left to catch up, just the two of us. I told him about the new guidebooks writing gigs I'd landed. More importantly though, I revealed that I'd pretty much finished up my first book and had possibly found a literary agent interested in representing me. He gave me an exuberant congratulations and I knew he meant every word. He also told me about his own book project that he was gradually working on—and suggested that we eventually swap publishing tips.

"I'm so glad that you've got all these great things happening for you!" he cheered. "I'd love to chat longer, but should really head to bed and actually there's something I need to tell you…"

Uggh… cue the drum roll for bad news… Jacob had started seeing this girl back in California and things were getting a little more serious.

One the one hand, I was very happy for him. It made sense to have something going on with a girl where he lived. If he was cutting 'physical' ties with me, it meant he really was serious about her. He was also upfront and honest. Dating a guy in a band sounds glamorous, but in reality, girls were constantly throwing themselves at musicians, so it required an incredible amount of trust.

On the other hand… he could have told me this before, by email! My instincts had been right after all. Sure, it had been great to see him and I always had fun at his concerts, but now the suburban trains were done and I was stuck out in the middle of nowhere. Double *merde* for me.

After his admission, he quickly changed the subject and we talked about Christmas holidays and other banal topics to end things on a light note. Then, he took me out to find a taxi. By some miracle there were actually taxis way out here. Thirty minutes and fifty Euros later (*Yikes! Not really a 'free' concert in the end*), I was tucked in at home, alone, save for a few lonely-hearts-club tears.

"At least he was honest... unlike *sommmme one* else!" consoled The Countess.

"Damn, so no more free concerts? And I missed the last one?" said Pussycat regretfully.

"Don't worry, dear. Jacob and I are still friends. I'm sure the next time he's over here on tour, we can wiggle our way onto more guest lists." As much as I was happy to know the truth, this was just a little too much truth (or too many surprise girlfriends!) for me to handle in two months' time.

"Well, never mind, we shall have a hearty cheers to ourselves for the new year then," suggested The Countess, popping another bottle of Domaine de Valentin. It was becoming an annual tradition: our little pre-holiday bubble fest.

"What was his last name again? I'm still annoyed you didn't invite me!" grumbled Rose, ever the lover of free things.

"Why do you want to know his last n... Hey! What are you doing??" I cried, reaching for her phone and almost spilling my champs on Pussycat in the process.

"Nothing! Don't fret, I won't put in a friend request for him or anything like that. I just wanted to know what he looked like," claimed Rose, scrolling through his Facebook profile.

"Good idea. I'll never get to see him in person if it involves going to a blaring concert. Pass it over!" tacked on The Countess, entering the creeper game. There was no point in trying to stop them now; I just had to pray they wouldn't do anything embarrassing.

"Yep, that's him," confirmed Pussycat, checking out Rose's phone screen.

"Not bad," approved Rose with a nod as she kept on scrolling down his page. "Hey, what's this? 'So glad we are getting to meet Cassandra at Christmas, after all this time!' Who's Cassandra?"

"Must be his girlfriend..." guessed Pussycat.

"But what's the 'all this time' about? I know Americans can have a different notion about size than we do over here in Europe. I wouldn't really categorize three or four months as 'a long time,' though," The Countess huffed with a dubious look on her face, a contagiously doubtful one.

"Give me that," I ordered, scooping the phone out of Rose's hands as fast as she'd done to me back in August. The comment seemed to be from an aunt or maybe his mom, obviously oblivious to Jacob's not so private Facebook page. I clicked in at the other comments.

"You guys make such a great couple!" I read with a smile. "You're proof of how a relationship can stand the test of such a long time and distance…"

My smile curved into a frown. The girls understood as soon as I had.

"Ummm, ahhh… more champagne?" fumbled The Countess, searching for a distraction.

"Stand the test of time? Sounds like more than three months to me!" exclaimed Pussycat.

"Honesty, huh? It appears to be a virtue *none* of these guys have," duly noted Rose.

"All I can say, is I'm honestly sick of them all. Countess, that new apartment you bought in Ireland… you said it's in a converted nunnery, right? Can I move in?"

"I think we're going to need to pass a larger order at the Domaine de Valentin booth at the next wine fair. Who's in?"

"Me!"

"*Moi aussi!*"

We cracked a third bottle and hoped the new year, if nothing else, would involve great times with the gals and with our special Valentin; the only 'le,' 'de,' 'il,' 'lui,' or 'ello' that would never fizzle out.

Or, who knows, maybe the fortune-tellers' destiny could come true in the coming year? No wait. I'd forgotten I'd left that cursed fate back in Vancouver.

I was now in charge of my own destiny, and happily so.

EPILOGUE

From: Viktor   Friday, December 23 2011 11:59 PM

Hey Lily,
Thanks so much for the birthday wishes - it reminded me
that I still haven't sent you a Christmas card!

It sounds like you have an action-packed new year. Any
time in NY is a good time, and if I know you, you will
make the most of it. I saw your name as an author of
Frommer's! Congratulations!

All the best for the new year, and here is hoping that I
make it over to see you sometime soon.

Xoxo Viktor

Want more Je T'Aime-ing? Turn the page!

More fun Je T'aime-ing is available on my site:
www.jetaimemeneither.com

And stay tuned for volume III of
Je T'Aime misadventures!

If you enjoyed this book, I'd be extremely grateful if you could leave a short review on either Amazon or Good Reads. It only takes a few minutes, but these are very helpful in advising and attracting potential readers. Or, simply help spread the word by telling your friends about the book!

ACKNOWLEDGEMENTS

The tales in this book would not have been possibly without Natasha Frid Finlay, Pascale Vincent Marquis and Paula McLean. It came together thanks to the hard work of my assiduous editor, Samatha Donaldson, the precious editorial assistance of Susan Romig McKee and Lauren Sarazen and the creativity of my talented cover designer Aurélie Dhuit. I am extremely grateful to test readers Corianna Heise, Wilma Hovius, Hannah Roberts Celik, Karin Bates, Bron Leslie and Shani Bauminger. Another important *merci* goes to photographer Rebecca Plotnick for my new author photo and Nicolas Beucher for the eBook formatting.

I would also like to thank my patient mother, the rest of my family who hasn't disowned me for my *oh la la!* Parisian behavior, Katrin Holt Dubreil, Heather Cowan Desportes, Clémence Malaret, Stefania Recchi, Heather Stimmler-Hall, Carolin C. Young, Riyako Suketomo, Gabie Demers, Sara McCarty, Nadia Scornaienchi, Kate Clarke, Vicki Lesage, Evelyne Rose, Kim Pegg, Gail Bosclair, Roxanne Frazer, the Canadian Ladies Group of Paris, Rachele Migliavacca, Marco Migliavacca, Brian Spence, Stephen Clarke, Ben Paneghel, Dimitri Gavaris, Jeremy Wolf, Mats Haglund, Romain Gil, Giancarlo Pizzi, Andrea, Il Cinghialo, Ruben, Justin A., L.O. M.W., H.V., P.R., S.S., and the gang of Cambridge Street. Another special mention goes to the birthday gals Tara and Clarisse as well as Jennifer Geraghty.

Finally, a *très grand merci* to all the readers of my books and blog, you truly help keep me writing!

ABOUT THE AUTHOR

April Lily Heise is a Paris-based Canadian writer and romance expert. When she isn't getting into romantic mischief, she writes on Paris, dating, culture and travel. Her writing has been featured in the Huffington Post, CondéNastTraveler.com, Business Insider, Frommer's, City Secrets, DK Eyewitness, WendyPerrin.com, among others. In addition to various travel guides, she is the author of *Je T'Aime, Me Neither*, the first book in the *Je T'Aime* Series. She also shares Paris tips, date ideas, dating stories and travel features on her blog www.jetaimemeneither.com.

64992962R00174

Made in the USA
Charleston, SC
11 December 2016